I0019981

Table of Contents

Chapter 1: Introduction to Web Design

Section 1.1: The Role of Web Design in Modern Business

In the fast-paced digital age, web design plays a pivotal role in shaping the success of businesses. A well-crafted online presence is often the first interaction potential customers have with a company. This section delves into the critical significance of web design in contemporary business strategies.

Web design extends beyond aesthetics; it serves as a powerful tool for brand representation and user engagement. The visual appeal of a website can leave a lasting impression, influencing users' perception of a brand's credibility and trustworthiness.

Moreover, web design directly impacts user experience (UX). An intuitive and user-friendly interface can enhance navigation, reduce bounce rates, and encourage users to explore further. Conversely, a poorly designed site can frustrate visitors and drive them away.

The Business Impact

In today's competitive landscape, businesses recognize that an effective online presence is vital for growth. A well-designed website can:

1. **Attract and Retain Customers:** A visually appealing site draws visitors in and encourages them to stay, increasing the chances of conversion.

2. **Build Trust:** A professional and polished website fosters trust, assuring users that the business is credible and reliable.

3. **Enhance Brand Identity:** Consistent design elements, such as logos and color schemes, reinforce brand identity and recognition.

4. **Improve Accessibility:** Well-designed websites are often more accessible to a broader audience, including users with disabilities.

Web Design as a Competitive Advantage

In a crowded marketplace, businesses that invest in web design gain a competitive edge. They can differentiate themselves from competitors, offer superior user experiences, and adapt to changing customer preferences.

Web design also aligns with other digital marketing strategies, such as search engine optimization (SEO) and content marketing. A well-structured website can improve SEO rankings, driving organic traffic and increasing visibility.

Evolving Trends

Web design is not static; it evolves alongside technological advancements and shifting design trends. Keeping abreast of these trends is essential for staying relevant and meeting user expectations. Some current trends include:

- **Mobile-First Design:** Given the prevalence of mobile devices, designing for mobile users first has become imperative.

- **Minimalism:** Clean, minimalist designs with ample white space are popular for their simplicity and focus on content.

- **Interactive Elements:** Incorporating interactive elements like animations and micro-interactions can engage users effectively.

- **Typography Experimentation:** Designers are exploring creative typography choices to add personality and uniqueness to websites.

- **Dark Mode:** The adoption of dark mode options for websites reduces eye strain and caters to user preferences.

In conclusion, web design is a dynamic and integral aspect of modern business operations. This section has provided an overview of its significance, impact, and evolving trends, setting the stage for a deeper exploration of web design principles and techniques in the subsequent chapters.

Section 1.2: The Web Design Process

The web design process is a structured approach that guides designers and developers through the creation of a website. It involves a series of steps, from conceptualization to deployment, ensuring that the final product aligns with business goals and user needs.

Understanding the Web Design Process

The web design process typically consists of the following phases:

1. **Planning:** This initial phase involves defining the project's objectives, target audience, and scope. It's crucial to gather requirements and establish a clear vision for the website.

2. **Research:** Research involves analyzing competitors' websites, industry trends, and user expectations. This information informs design decisions and ensures the site's competitiveness.

3. **Wireframing:** Wireframes are basic, skeletal layouts that outline the site's structure and content placement. They serve as a visual guide for the site's layout and functionality.

4. **Design:** Design encompasses both visual and user experience design. Visual design focuses on aesthetics, including color schemes, typography, and graphics. User experience design prioritizes usability, navigation, and interaction.

5. **Development:** During this phase, developers translate the design into code. HTML, CSS, and JavaScript are used to build the site's structure, style, and functionality.

6. **Testing:** Thorough testing is essential to identify and rectify any issues. This includes checking for cross-browser compatibility, responsiveness, and functionality.

7. **Review and Feedback:** Clients and stakeholders review the website and provide feedback. Iterations and revisions are made based on this feedback.

8. **Launch:** After rigorous testing and refinement, the website is ready for deployment. This involves setting up hosting, configuring domains, and making the site live.

9. **Post-launch Maintenance:** Websites require ongoing maintenance to ensure they remain functional, secure, and up-to-date. Regular updates, backups, and security measures are essential.

The Role of Collaboration

Effective web design often involves collaboration between designers, developers, content creators, and stakeholders. Clear communication and collaboration are vital to ensure that the design aligns with the project's goals and meets user expectations.

```html
<!-- Example of Collaboration in HTML -->
<div class="collaboration">
    <img src="designer.png" alt="Designer">
    <img src="developer.png" alt="Developer">
    <img src="content-creator.png" alt="Content Creator">
    <img src="stakeholder.png" alt="Stakeholder">
</div>
```

Agile and Waterfall Approaches

Two common methodologies for web design projects are Agile and Waterfall:

- **Agile:** Agile emphasizes flexibility and iterative development. It involves breaking the project into smaller tasks and continuously refining the product based on feedback. This approach suits projects with evolving requirements.

- **Waterfall:** Waterfall is a more traditional, sequential approach. It follows a linear progression from planning to deployment. It's suitable for projects with well-defined requirements.

Tools for Web Design

Web designers and developers use a variety of tools to streamline the design process. These include design software (e.g., Adobe XD, Sketch), code editors (e.g., Visual Studio Code, Sublime Text), version control systems (e.g., Git), and project management platforms (e.g., Trello, Asana).

In summary, the web design process is a structured journey from planning to deployment, involving various phases, collaboration, and methodologies. Successful web design combines aesthetics and functionality while meeting user needs and business objectives.

Section 1.3: Key Technologies: HTML, CSS, JavaScript, and JQuery

Web design relies on a set of core technologies that enable the creation of dynamic and visually appealing websites. Understanding these technologies is fundamental to becoming a proficient web designer.

HTML (Hypertext Markup Language)

HTML is the backbone of web content. It provides the structure and semantics of a web page, defining headings, paragraphs, links, and other elements. HTML5, the latest version of HTML, introduced several enhancements for multimedia, semantic markup, and form handling.

Here's a simple HTML example:

```html
<!DOCTYPE html>
<html>
<head>
    <title>My Web Page</title>
</head>
<body>
    <h1>Welcome to My Web Page</h1>
    <p>This is a sample paragraph.</p>
    <a href="https://www.example.com">Visit Example.com</a>
</body>
</html>
```

CSS (Cascading Style Sheets)

CSS is responsible for styling and layout. It allows designers to control the visual appearance of web elements, including colors, fonts, spacing, and positioning. CSS3 introduced advanced features like animations and transitions.

Here's a basic CSS example:

```css
/* CSS Styles */
body {
    font-family: Arial, sans-serif;
    background-color: #f0f0f0;
}

h1 {
    color: #333;
}

p {
    font-size: 16px;
}
```

```css
a {
    text-decoration: none;
    color: #0077cc;
}
```

JavaScript

JavaScript adds interactivity and dynamic behavior to web pages. It can respond to user actions, manipulate the DOM, and make asynchronous requests to servers. JavaScript is essential for creating features like form validation, interactive maps, and image sliders.

Here's a simple JavaScript snippet:

```javascript
// JavaScript Code
function greetUser() {
    let userName = prompt("Enter your name:");
    alert(`Hello, ${userName}! Welcome to our website.`);
}
```

JQuery

jQuery is a popular JavaScript library that simplifies DOM manipulation and event handling. It streamlines complex tasks and ensures cross-browser compatibility. While its usage has declined with the advancements in modern JavaScript, it remains relevant in certain scenarios.

Here's an example of using jQuery to handle a click event:

```html
<!-- HTML with jQuery -->
<button id="myButton">Click Me</button>

<script src="https://code.jquery.com/jquery-3.6.0.min.js"></script>
<script>
    $(document).ready(function() {
        $("#myButton").click(function() {
            alert("Button clicked!");
        });
    });
</script>
```

These technologies—HTML, CSS, JavaScript, and jQuery—form the foundation of web design. As you delve deeper into web design, you'll explore how these technologies work together to create engaging and functional web experiences.

Section 1.4: Setting Up Your Web Development Environment

Before diving into web design, it's essential to set up a proper web development environment. An efficient environment ensures you can work seamlessly, experiment with code, and test your designs effectively.

Choosing a Text Editor or Integrated Development Environment (IDE)

Selecting the right text editor or IDE is one of the first steps in setting up your web development environment. Some popular options include:

- **Visual Studio Code (VSCode):** A free, open-source code editor developed by Microsoft. VSCode offers a vast library of extensions for web development.

- **Sublime Text:** A lightweight and highly customizable text editor known for its speed and simplicity.

- **Atom:** Another open-source code editor that's highly extensible and user-friendly.

- **WebStorm:** An IDE specifically designed for web development, offering advanced features for JavaScript, HTML, and CSS.

Installing Required Software

Your web development environment will depend on the technologies you plan to use. However, here are some common software components you may need to install:

1. **Web Browsers:** Ensure you have multiple web browsers installed for testing and debugging. Popular choices include Google Chrome, Mozilla Firefox, and Microsoft Edge.

2. **Node.js:** If you're working with JavaScript, Node.js is essential. It allows you to run JavaScript on the server and includes npm, a package manager for web development libraries and tools.

3. **Version Control:** Consider using a version control system like Git. Platforms like GitHub or GitLab can help you collaborate and manage your code.

4. **Local Development Server:** Depending on your project, you may need a local development server to run your web applications. Tools like Apache, Nginx, or simple Python HTTP servers can serve this purpose.

Organizing Your Project Structure

Maintaining a well-organized project structure is crucial for efficient web development. Here's a common structure for a web project:

```
my-web-project/
|
```

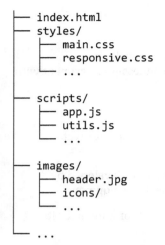

```
├── index.html
├── styles/
│   ├── main.css
│   ├── responsive.css
│   └── ...
│
├── scripts/
│   ├── app.js
│   ├── utils.js
│   └── ...
│
├── images/
│   ├── header.jpg
│   ├── icons/
│   └── ...
│
└── ...
```

This structure separates HTML, CSS, JavaScript, and other assets into distinct directories, making it easier to manage and collaborate with others.

Setting Up a Code Editor

Once you've chosen a code editor or IDE, you can customize it to enhance your productivity. Common customizations include:

- **Extensions:** Install extensions or plugins that provide features like code autocompletion, linting, and integration with version control systems.

- **Themes:** Choose a coding theme that suits your preferences. Many themes offer light and dark mode options.

- **Keyboard Shortcuts:** Familiarize yourself with keyboard shortcuts to streamline your coding tasks.

- **Workspace Configuration:** Configure your editor to match your project's requirements. This may include setting up indentation, tab size, and file associations.

Testing Your Environment

After setting up your web development environment, it's essential to verify that everything is functioning correctly. Create a simple "Hello, World!" HTML file, apply some basic styling, and add a JavaScript function to display an alert. Open this file in your chosen web browser to ensure it renders as expected and that your code editor provides real-time feedback.

A well-configured web development environment is your toolkit for building and designing websites effectively. Taking the time to set it up correctly will save you time and streamline your workflow as you embark on your web design journey.

Section 1.5: Web Design Trends and Inspirations

In the ever-evolving field of web design, staying informed about the latest trends and drawing inspiration from existing designs is essential. This section explores the importance of keeping up with trends and finding creative inspiration.

Why Follow Web Design Trends?

Web design trends are not just about aesthetics; they often reflect changes in user behavior, technology, and design philosophy. Here are some reasons why keeping up with trends is crucial:

1. **User Expectations:** Users expect modern, visually appealing, and intuitive websites. Adhering to current trends can help meet these expectations.

2. **Competitive Advantage:** Staying ahead of the curve can give your websites a competitive edge, making them stand out in the crowded digital landscape.

3. **Improved User Experience:** Many trends focus on enhancing user experience, which can lead to lower bounce rates and higher engagement.

4. **Responsive Design:** Trends often align with responsive design principles, ensuring your websites look and function well on various devices.

5. **Innovation:** Trends drive innovation in design and technology. By embracing trends, you can experiment with new techniques and approaches.

Key Web Design Trends

While web design trends evolve, several recurring themes have emerged in recent years:

1. **Minimalism:** Minimalist design emphasizes simplicity, clean lines, and ample white space. It focuses on essential elements, reducing clutter.

2. **Mobile-First Design:** Given the prevalence of mobile devices, designing for mobile users first has become a standard practice.

3. **Typography:** Creative typography choices, including custom fonts and font pairings, can add personality and uniqueness to websites.

4. **Micro-Interactions:** Subtle animations and micro-interactions enhance user engagement by providing feedback and visual cues.

5. **Dark Mode:** Dark mode options reduce eye strain and cater to user preferences, especially in applications that are used for extended periods.

6. **3D Elements:** Three-dimensional visuals and effects can create depth and immersive experiences.

7. **Illustrations and Hand-Drawn Art:** Custom illustrations and hand-drawn elements can give websites a distinctive, human touch.

8. **Voice User Interfaces (VUIs):** As voice-controlled devices become more common, designing for VUIs is gaining importance.

9. **Accessibility:** An increasing focus on inclusive design ensures that websites are usable by individuals with disabilities.

Finding Inspiration

Drawing inspiration is a crucial part of the design process. Here are some ways to find inspiration:

- **Browse Award-Winning Websites:** Explore websites that have won design awards to see cutting-edge design in action.

- **Design Galleries:** Websites like Behance, Awwwards, and Dribbble showcase innovative designs from around the world.

- **Competitor Analysis:** Analyze the websites of competitors and industry leaders to identify trends and best practices.

- **Nature and Art:** Sometimes, inspiration comes from the world outside of web design. Nature, art, and everyday life can spark creative ideas.

- **User Feedback:** Listen to user feedback and observations to identify areas for improvement and innovation.

- **Experimentation:** Don't be afraid to experiment and push the boundaries of design. Some of the most innovative designs come from taking risks.

In conclusion, web design is a dynamic field that constantly evolves. By staying informed about trends and finding inspiration, you can create websites that not only meet user expectations but also push the boundaries of design innovation. Embracing change and creativity are key to success in web design.

Chapter 2: HTML Fundamentals

Section 2.1: Introduction to HTML Markup

HTML (Hypertext Markup Language) is the foundational language of the web. It provides the structure and content for web pages, allowing you to define headings, paragraphs, links, images, forms, and more. In this section, we'll delve into the basics of HTML markup and how it forms the building blocks of web content.

HTML Document Structure

An HTML document follows a hierarchical structure. It typically consists of the following elements:

```html
<!DOCTYPE html>
<html>
<head>
    <!-- Metadata, such as the page title and character set -->
    <meta charset="UTF-8">
    <title>My Web Page</title>
</head>
<body>
    <!-- Content of the web page -->
    <header>
        <h1>Welcome to My Web Page</h1>
    </header>
    <nav>
        <ul>
            <li><a href="#section1">Section 1</a></li>
            <li><a href="#section2">Section 2</a></li>
            <!-- More navigation links -->
        </ul>
    </nav>
    <main>
        <section id="section1">
            <h2>Section 1</h2>
            <p>This is the content of Section 1.</p>
        </section>
        <section id="section2">
            <h2>Section 2</h2>
            <p>This is the content of Section 2.</p>
        </section>
        <!-- More sections and content -->
    </main>
    <footer>
        <p>&copy; 2023 My Web Page</p>
    </footer>
```

```
</body>
</html>
```

- `<!DOCTYPE html>`: This declaration defines the document type and version of HTML being used (HTML5 in this case).

- `<html>`: The root element that encloses the entire HTML document.

- `<head>`: Contains metadata about the document, including the page title and character set.

- `<body>`: Houses the visible content of the web page, including headings, paragraphs, navigation, and more.

HTML Elements and Tags

HTML consists of elements, which are enclosed by tags. Tags are typically written in pairs: an opening tag and a closing tag. Here are some commonly used HTML elements:

- `<h1>`, `<h2>`, `<h3>`, ... `<h6>`: Headings of different levels, where `<h1>` is the highest level and `<h6>` is the lowest.

- `<p>`: Defines a paragraph of text.

- `<a>`: Creates hyperlinks to other web pages or resources.

- `<ul>`: Defines an unordered (bulleted) list.

- `<ol>`: Defines an ordered (numbered) list.

- `<li>`: Represents a list item within `<ul>` or `<ol>`.

Adding Attributes

HTML elements often include attributes that provide additional information or settings. For example:

```
<a href="https://www.example.com" target="_blank">Visit Example.com</a>
```

- `href`: Specifies the destination URL for the hyperlink.

- `target="_blank"`: Opens the link in a new browser tab or window.

Nesting Elements

HTML elements can be nested within one another to create complex structures. For instance:

```
<ul>
    <li>Item 1</li>
    <li>Item 2</li>
```

```
    <li>Item 3</li>
</ul>
```

Here, the `<ul>` element contains three `<li>` elements to create a bulleted list.

Understanding HTML markup is the foundation of web design. In the following sections, we'll explore HTML5's semantic elements, text formatting, links, and accessibility features in more detail, allowing you to create well-structured and user-friendly web content.

Section 2.2: Document Structure with HTML5

HTML5 introduced a set of semantic elements that provide more meaningful and structured ways to define the content and layout of web pages. In this section, we'll explore some of the key HTML5 semantic elements and their roles in structuring web documents.

The Importance of Semantic Elements

Semantic elements are tags that carry meaning about the content they enclose. They help both web browsers and developers understand the purpose and context of various parts of a web page. Using semantic elements improves the accessibility, SEO, and maintainability of your web pages.

Header and Footer

The `<header>` and `<footer>` elements define the header and footer sections of a web page, respectively. These sections often contain information such as logos, navigation menus, copyright notices, and contact details.

```
<header>
    <h1>My Website</h1>
    <nav>
        <ul>
            <li><a href="#home">Home</a></li>
            <li><a href="#about">About</a></li>
            <!-- More navigation links -->
        </ul>
    </nav>
</header>

<footer>
    <p>&copy; 2023 My Website</p>
</footer>
```

Navigation

The `<nav>` element is used to define navigation menus, making it easier for screen readers and search engines to identify and interpret navigation links.

```
<nav>
    <ul>
        <li><a href="#home">Home</a></li>
        <li><a href="#about">About</a></li>
        <!-- More navigation links -->
    </ul>
</nav>
```

Main Content

The `<main>` element represents the main content of a web page. Each page should have only one `<main>` element, and it should encapsulate the primary content of the page.

```
<main>
    <h1>Welcome to Our Blog</h1>
    <article>
        <h2>Article Title</h2>
        <p>Article content goes here...</p>
    </article>
    <!-- More articles or content -->
</main>
```

Section and Article

The `<section>` and `<article>` elements are used to divide the content of a web page into meaningful sections. `<section>` is a generic container, while `<article>` is used for self-contained content, such as blog posts or news articles.

```
<section>
    <h2>Web Development</h2>
    <p>Learn about HTML, CSS, and JavaScript.</p>
</section>

<article>
    <h2>How to Build a Responsive Website</h2>
    <p>Step-by-step guide to creating responsive web designs.</p>
</article>
```

Aside

The `<aside>` element is used for content that is tangentially related to the main content, such as sidebars, pull quotes, or advertising.

```
<aside>
    <h3>Related Links</h3>
    <ul>
        <li><a href="#article1">Read More</a></li>
        <li><a href="#article2">Other Articles</a></li>
    </ul>
</aside>
```

Figure and Figcaption

The `<figure>` and `<figcaption>` elements are used to associate captions with images and other media elements.

```
<figure>
    <img src="image.jpg" alt="An example image">
    <figcaption>Caption for the image.</figcaption>
</figure>
```

By incorporating these HTML5 semantic elements into your web pages, you can create well-structured and accessible content that improves both the user experience and search engine optimization. Understanding how to use these elements effectively is an essential skill for web designers and developers.

Section 2.3: Working with Headings, Paragraphs, and Text

Headings, paragraphs, and text are fundamental elements in HTML that allow you to structure and convey content effectively. In this section, we'll explore how to work with these elements to create well-organized and readable web pages.

Headings

HTML provides six levels of headings, from `<h1>` (the highest level) to `<h6>` (the lowest level). Headings are used to define the hierarchy and structure of content on a page.

```
<h1>Main Heading</h1>
<h2>Subheading 1</h2>
<p>Paragraph of text here...</p>
<h2>Subheading 2</h2>
<p>Another paragraph of text...</p>
```

- Use `<h1>` for the main title or heading of your page.

- Use lower-level headings (e.g., `<h2>`, `<h3>`) for subsections within your content.

- Avoid skipping heading levels (e.g., jumping from `<h2>` to `<h4>`), as it can lead to confusion for both users and search engines.

Paragraphs

The `<p>` element is used to define paragraphs of text. It automatically adds spacing between paragraphs for better readability.

```
<p>This is a paragraph of text. It can contain multiple sentences and provide information or context.</p>
<p>Another paragraph follows, creating separation and clarity in the content.</p>
```

- Always use `<p>` elements for text paragraphs to maintain proper structure and formatting.

- Avoid using multiple `<br>` (line break) tags to create paragraphs, as it is not semantically correct.

HTML provides several elements to format and emphasize text:

- `<em>` (emphasis): Renders text in italics, typically used to convey subtle emphasis.

```
<p>This is <em>important</em> information.</p>
```

- `<strong>`: Renders text in bold, indicating strong emphasis or importance.

```
<p><strong>Warning:</strong> This action cannot be undone.</p>
```

- `<mark>`: Highlights text with a background color, useful for indicating search results or specific terms.

```
<p>Search for <mark>web design</mark> courses.</p>
```

- `<abbr>` (abbreviation): Defines an abbreviation or acronym, providing a tooltip with the full expansion.

```
<p><abbr title="World Wide Web">WWW</abbr> is an essential part of the
internet.</p>
```

- `<code>`: Renders text as code, suitable for displaying programming code or commands.

```
<p>To print a message in Python, use <code>print("Hello, World!")</code>.</p>
```

- `<blockquote>`: Indicates a block of text that is a quotation from another source. It is often styled with indentation or other formatting.

```
<blockquote>
    <p>It does not matter how slowly you go as long as you do not stop.</p>
    <cite>Confucius</cite>
</blockquote>
```

- `<cite>`: Identifies the source of a quotation within a `<blockquote>`.

These formatting elements help you convey meaning, emphasize important points, and provide context within your content.

By using headings, paragraphs, and text formatting effectively, you can create web pages that are easy to read, understand, and navigate, enhancing the user experience and accessibility of your content.

Section 2.4: Lists, Links, and Anchors

HTML provides several elements for creating lists, defining hyperlinks, and using anchors to navigate within a web page or to external resources. In this section, we'll explore how to use these elements to enhance the structure and interactivity of your web pages.

Unordered Lists (<ul>) and List Items (<li>)

Unordered lists are created using the <ul> element, and list items within the list are defined using the <li> element. Unordered lists are typically used for items without a specific order, such as bullet-point lists.

```
<ul>
    <li>Item 1</li>
    <li>Item 2</li>
    <li>Item 3</li>
</ul>
```

Ordered Lists (<ol>) and List Items (<li>)

Ordered lists are similar to unordered lists but are used for items with a specific order or sequence. They are created using the <ol> element.

```
<ol>
    <li>Step 1</li>
    <li>Step 2</li>
    <li>Step 3</li>
</ol>
```

Nested Lists

You can nest lists within other lists to create more complex structures. For example, you can create a nested unordered list within an ordered list:

```
<ol>
    <li>Main item 1</li>
    <li>Main item 2
        <ul>
            <li>Subitem 1</li>
            <li>Subitem 2</li>
        </ul>
    </li>
    <li>Main item 3</li>
</ol>
```

Hyperlinks (`<a>`)

Hyperlinks, defined using the `<a>` (anchor) element, allow you to link to other web pages, resources, or sections within the same page. You specify the link's destination using the `href` attribute.

```html
<a href="https://www.example.com">Visit Example.com</a>
```

Anchor Links

To create internal links within the same page, you can use anchor links. These links reference an element on the page by its `id` attribute. Anchor links are useful for creating navigation menus or linking to specific sections of a long web page.

```html
<!-- Creating an anchor link -->
<a href="#section1">Jump to Section 1</a>

<!-- Defining a section with an id -->
<section id="section1">
    <h2>Section 1</h2>
    <p>This is the content of Section 1.</p>
</section>
```

Linking to Email Addresses

You can use the `mailto:` scheme to create links that open the user's default email client with a pre-filled email address.

```html
<a href="mailto:contact@example.com">Contact Us</a>
```

Linking to Files

You can link to various types of files, such as PDFs, documents, or images, by specifying the file's path in the `href` attribute.

```html
<a href="documents/document.pdf">Download PDF</a>
```

Opening Links in a New Tab

To open a link in a new browser tab or window, you can use the `target="_blank"` attribute.

```html
<a href="https://www.example.com" target="_blank">Visit Example.com</a>
```

By mastering lists, links, and anchors, you can create well-structured and interconnected web pages that provide a smooth and informative user experience. These elements are essential for navigation, content organization, and user engagement on the web.

Section 2.5: Semantic HTML Elements and Accessibility

Semantic HTML elements play a crucial role in web design and development. They not only help structure your content logically but also enhance the accessibility of your web pages. In this section, we'll explore the importance of semantic HTML elements and how they contribute to making your websites more inclusive.

What Are Semantic HTML Elements?

Semantic HTML elements are tags that carry meaning about the type of content they enclose. Instead of using generic <div> and <span> elements for everything, you should use semantic elements to describe the purpose and significance of the content.

For example, instead of using a <div> to represent a navigation menu, you can use the <nav> element:

```
<!-- Non-semantic -->
<div class="menu">
    <ul>
        <li><a href="#">Home</a></li>
        <li><a href="#">About</a></li>
        <!-- More menu items -->
    </ul>
</div>

<!-- Semantic -->
<nav>
    <ul>
        <li><a href="#">Home</a></li>
        <li><a href="#">About</a></li>
        <!-- More menu items -->
    </ul>
</nav>
```

Benefits of Semantic HTML

1. **Improved Accessibility:** Screen readers and assistive technologies rely on semantic HTML to understand and interpret web content. Using semantic elements makes your website more accessible to people with disabilities.

2. **SEO-Friendly:** Search engines also benefit from semantic HTML, as they can better understand the content and context of your pages. This can improve your website's search engine rankings.

3. **Ease of Maintenance:** Semantic HTML makes your code more self-explanatory, which makes it easier to maintain and collaborate on web projects.

4. **Consistency:** Semantic elements provide consistency in web design, making it easier for designers and developers to work together and follow best practices.

Common Semantic Elements

Here are some of the most commonly used semantic HTML elements:

- `<header>`: Represents the header of a section or the entire page.
- `<nav>`: Defines navigation menus.
- `<main>`: Represents the main content of the page.
- `<article>`: Defines a self-contained piece of content, such as a blog post.
- `<section>`: Represents a thematic grouping of content.
- `<aside>`: Represents content that is related but not central to the main content.
- `<footer>`: Represents the footer of a section or the entire page.

Accessibility Considerations

When using semantic elements, it's important to consider accessibility:

1. **Alt Text for Images:** Always provide descriptive alt text for images to ensure that users with visual impairments can understand the content.

2. **Heading Structure:** Use headings in a hierarchical and logical order (`<h1>` to `<h6>`) to outline the structure of your content.

3. **Labels for Forms:** Use `<label>` elements with the for attribute to associate labels with form fields for screen reader users.

4. **Keyboard Navigation:** Ensure that all interactive elements, such as links and buttons, can be navigated and activated using a keyboard.

5. **Testing with Assistive Technologies:** Regularly test your website with screen readers and other assistive technologies to identify and address accessibility issues.

By incorporating semantic HTML elements and adhering to accessibility best practices, you can create websites that are not only visually appealing but also inclusive and user-friendly, catering to a broader audience.

Chapter 3: CSS Styling

Section 3.1: Understanding CSS and Stylesheets

Cascading Style Sheets (CSS) is a fundamental technology in web design that allows you to control the presentation and layout of web content. In this section, we'll explore the basics of CSS, its role in web design, and how to use stylesheets to apply consistent and visually appealing styles to your web pages.

What is CSS?

CSS is a style sheet language used to describe the presentation of HTML and XML documents. It defines how elements on a web page should be displayed, including their colors, fonts, sizes, spacing, and positioning. CSS separates the structure (defined by HTML) from the presentation (defined by CSS), allowing for greater flexibility and maintainability in web design.

How CSS Works

CSS operates on a simple principle: it selects HTML elements and applies styles to them. These styles are defined in rules within a stylesheet. Each rule consists of a selector and a declaration block enclosed in curly braces. Here's a basic example:

```css
/* CSS Comment */
selector {
    property: value;
}
```

- **Selector:** Specifies the HTML elements to which the styles should be applied. For example, h1 selects all <h1> elements, and .class selects elements with a specific class, while #id selects an element with a specific ID.

- **Property:** Indicates the aspect of the selected element you want to style, such as color, font-size, or margin.

- **Value:** Specifies the value for the property, like red, 16px, or 2em.

Including CSS in HTML

You can include CSS styles in an HTML document using the <style> element within the document's <head> section or by linking to an external CSS file using the <link> element. Here's how to use both methods:

Inline Styles

```html
<!DOCTYPE html>
<html>
<head>
    <title>My Web Page</title>
```

```
<style>
    /* Inline CSS */
    h1 {
        color: blue;
        font-size: 24px;
    }
</style>
</head>
<body>
    <h1>Welcome to My Web Page</h1>
    <p>This is some text.</p>
</body>
</html>
```

External Stylesheet
```
<!DOCTYPE html>
<html>
<head>
    <title>My Web Page</title>
    <link rel="stylesheet" type="text/css" href="styles.css">
</head>
<body>
    <h1>Welcome to My Web Page</h1>
    <p>This is some text.</p>
</body>
</html>
```

Cascading and Specificity

The "C" in CSS stands for "cascading," which refers to the order in which styles are applied when there are conflicting rules. CSS rules can have different levels of specificity, and more specific rules override less specific ones. Understanding specificity is crucial for resolving styling conflicts.

Inheritance

CSS styles can be inherited from parent elements to their children. For example, if you set a font style on a <div>, it may apply to all the text within that <div> and its child elements, unless overridden by more specific styles.

CSS Comments

You can add comments to your CSS code using /* */. Comments are not displayed on the web page but are helpful for documenting your styles.

```
/* This is a CSS comment */
selector {
    property: value; /* This is another comment */
}
```

Conclusion

CSS is a powerful tool for controlling the visual aspects of web pages. By understanding how CSS works and how to apply styles to HTML elements, you can create web designs that are visually appealing and user-friendly. In the following sections, we'll dive deeper into CSS selectors, style rules, and various aspects of web page styling.

Section 3.2: Selectors and Style Rules

Selectors and style rules are fundamental concepts in CSS that allow you to target specific HTML elements and apply styles to them. In this section, we'll explore different types of selectors and how to create style rules to customize the appearance of your web pages.

CSS Selectors

Selectors are patterns that identify which HTML elements to style. CSS provides various types of selectors to target elements based on different criteria:

1. Element Selector

An element selector targets all instances of a specific HTML element. For example, to select all <p> (paragraph) elements:

```css
p {
    /* Styles applied to all paragraphs */
    font-size: 16px;
    color: #333;
}
```

2. Class Selector

A class selector selects elements with a specific class attribute. You define the class in your HTML and apply it to one or more elements. Class selectors are prefixed with a dot (.).

```html
<!-- HTML -->
<p class="highlight">This paragraph has a class.</p>
```

```css
/* CSS */
.highlight {
    /* Styles applied to elements with class="highlight" */
    background-color: yellow;
}
```

3. ID Selector

An ID selector selects a single element with a specific ID attribute. IDs should be unique within a document. ID selectors are prefixed with a hash (#).

```
<!-- HTML -->
<div id="header">Header Content</div>

/* CSS */
#header {
    /* Styles applied to the element with id="header" */
    font-size: 24px;
    color: blue;
}
```

4. Descendant Selector

A descendant selector selects an element that is a descendant of another element. It is used to target elements within a specific context.

```
<!-- HTML -->
<div class="container">
    <p>This is a paragraph inside a container.</p>
</div>

/* CSS */
.container p {
    /* Styles applied to <p> elements inside elements with class="container"
*/
    margin: 10px;
}
```

5. Child Selector

A child selector selects an element that is a direct child of another element. It is denoted using the > symbol.

```
<!-- HTML -->
<ul>
    <li>List item 1</li>
    <li>List item 2</li>
</ul>

/* CSS */
ul > li {
    /* Styles applied to <li> elements that are direct children of <ul> */
    list-style-type: square;
}
```

6. Attribute Selector

An attribute selector targets elements with a specific attribute and optional attribute values. For example, to select all <a> elements with a target="_blank" attribute:

```
a[target="_blank"] {
    /* Styles applied to <a> elements with target="_blank" attribute */
```

```
    text-decoration: underline;
}
```

Style Rules

A style rule consists of a selector and a declaration block enclosed in curly braces {}. The declaration block contains one or more property-value pairs, separated by semicolons ;.

```
/* Selector */
h1 {
    /* Declaration Block */
    font-size: 24px;
    color: #333;
}
```

- **Selector:** Specifies which elements the style rule applies to.

- **Declaration Block:** Contains the styles to be applied to the selected elements.

Understanding selectors and creating effective style rules is essential for customizing the appearance of your web pages. In the next sections, we'll delve into various CSS properties and values to further enhance your web design skills.

Section 3.3: Formatting Text and Typography

Text formatting and typography are critical aspects of web design that greatly influence the readability and visual appeal of your content. In this section, we'll explore how CSS allows you to style text, set fonts, and control typographic elements on your web pages.

Font Properties

1. font-family

The font-family property defines the font or list of fonts to be used for rendering text. You can specify a generic font family (e.g., "sans-serif" or "serif") or provide a specific font name. The browser will use the first available font from the list.

```
body {
    font-family: Arial, Helvetica, sans-serif;
}
```

2. font-size

The font-size property determines the size of the text. You can use various units, such as pixels (px), points (pt), or percentages (%).

```
h1 {
    font-size: 24px;
}
```

```
p {
    font-size: 16px;
}
```

3. font-weight

The font-weight property controls the thickness or boldness of the text. You can use values like "normal," "bold," or numeric values for finer control.

```
strong {
    font-weight: bold;
}
```

```
span {
    font-weight: 600; /* Numeric value for bold */
}
```

4. font-style

The font-style property defines whether the text is italic, oblique, or normal (default).

```
em {
    font-style: italic;
}
```

5. text-transform

The text-transform property allows you to change the capitalization of text. Common values include "uppercase," "lowercase," and "capitalize."

```
button {
    text-transform: uppercase;
}
```

6. line-height

The line-height property controls the spacing between lines of text. It can improve readability and aesthetics.

```
p {
    line-height: 1.5; /* Relative to the font size */
}
```

Text Color and Background

1. color

The color property sets the text color. You can use color names, hexadecimal values, RGB values, or HSL values.

```
h2 {
    color: #007acc; /* Hexadecimal color */
}

blockquote {
    color: rgba(0, 128, 0, 0.8); /* RGBA color */
}
```

2. background-color

The `background-color` property defines the background color behind text or elements.

```
button {
    background-color: #ff9900;
}
```

Text Decoration

1. text-decoration

The `text-decoration` property controls text decoration, such as underlines, overlines, and line-throughs.

```
a {
    text-decoration: underline;
}
```

```
del {
    text-decoration: line-through;
}
```

Letter Spacing and Word Spacing

1. letter-spacing

The `letter-spacing` property adjusts the space between individual characters.

```
h3 {
    letter-spacing: 1px;
}
```

2. word-spacing

The `word-spacing` property modifies the space between words.

```
p {
    word-spacing: 2px;
}
```

Text Shadows

1. text-shadow

The `text-shadow` property adds shadows to text. It takes values for horizontal and vertical offsets, blur radius, and shadow color.

```
h1 {
    text-shadow: 2px 2px 4px rgba(0, 0, 0, 0.5);
}
```

Typography and text formatting are powerful tools for creating visually appealing and readable web content. By understanding and using these CSS properties effectively, you can enhance the overall design and user experience of your web pages. In the following sections, we'll delve deeper into controlling colors, backgrounds, and layouts using CSS.

Section 3.4: Managing Colors and Backgrounds

Colors and backgrounds play a crucial role in web design, as they contribute to the overall visual appeal and aesthetics of a web page. In this section, we'll delve into CSS properties and techniques for managing colors and backgrounds to create visually engaging and harmonious web designs.

Setting Text Color

The `color` property is used to set the color of text within HTML elements. You can specify colors using various methods:

- Color names: CSS recognizes common color names like "red," "blue," "green," etc.
- Hexadecimal values: Represented as #RRGGBB, where RR, GG, and BB are hexadecimal values for the red, green, and blue channels, respectively.
- RGB values: Represented as rgb(R, G, B), where R, G, and B are integers between 0 and 255.
- RGBA values: Similar to RGB but with an additional alpha channel that controls opacity, represented as rgba(R, G, B, A) where A is a value between 0 (completely transparent) and 1 (fully opaque).

```
/* Setting text color using color names */
h1 {
    color: red;
}

/* Setting text color using hexadecimal value */
p {
    color: #336699;
}

/* Setting text color using RGB value */
```

```css
a {
    color: rgb(255, 0, 0);
}

/* Setting text color using RGBA value with transparency */
span {
    color: rgba(0, 128, 0, 0.5);
}
```

Background Colors

The `background-color` property is used to set the background color of HTML elements. It follows the same color representation methods as the `color` property.

```css
/* Setting background color using color names */
button {
    background-color: yellow;
}

/* Setting background color using hexadecimal value */
div {
    background-color: #f0f0f0;
}

/* Setting background color using RGBA value with transparency */
section {
    background-color: rgba(0, 0, 255, 0.2);
}
```

Gradient Backgrounds

CSS allows you to create gradient backgrounds using the `linear-gradient` and `radial-gradient` functions. These gradients can be used as background images.

```css
/* Linear gradient background */
.header {
    background-image: linear-gradient(to bottom, #ff9900, #ffcc00);
}

/* Radial gradient background */
.button {
    background-image: radial-gradient(circle, #3399ff, #0066cc);
}
```

Background Images

You can use images as backgrounds by specifying the image URL with the `background-image` property. Additionally, you can control properties like background size, repeat, and position.

```css
/* Using an image as a background */
.banner {
    background-image: url('image.jpg');
    background-size: cover; /* Cover the entire element */
    background-repeat: no-repeat; /* Do not repeat the image */
    background-position: center; /* Center the image */
}
```

CSS Gradients vs. Background Images

CSS gradients are often preferred over background images for several reasons:

- They can be created dynamically and don't require additional HTTP requests.
- They can be resized and adjusted easily.
- They can be more performant, especially for simple backgrounds.

However, background images are still valuable for complex or highly detailed backgrounds.

Transparency and Opacity

As mentioned earlier, you can control transparency using RGBA values. Additionally, you can use the opacity property to control the overall opacity of an element and its contents.

```css
/* Setting overall opacity */
.overlay {
    opacity: 0.8; /* Value between 0 (transparent) and 1 (fully opaque) */
}
```

Background Size and Position

The background-size property allows you to control how a background image is sized and scaled. You can specify values like cover, contain, or specific dimensions.

```css
/* Background size property */
.header {
    background-size: cover; /* Scales the image to cover the entire element */
}
```

```css
/* Background position property */
.button {
    background-position: center top; /* Positions the image at the center top of the element */
}
```

Understanding how to manage colors and backgrounds is essential for creating visually appealing web designs. These CSS properties and techniques provide you with the tools to customize the look and feel of your web pages and enhance the user experience. In the following sections, we'll explore layouts and positioning using CSS.

Section 3.5: Layouts and Positioning with CSS

Creating effective layouts and controlling the positioning of elements on a web page is a fundamental aspect of web design. CSS provides various techniques and properties to achieve responsive and visually appealing layouts. In this section, we'll explore layout concepts, positioning, and CSS properties that facilitate layout design.

CSS Display Property

The `display` property specifies how an element should be displayed. Common values include:

- block: Renders the element as a block-level element, taking up the full width available and stacking vertically. Example: `<div>`, `<p>`.
- inline: Renders the element as an inline-level element, allowing it to flow within the content. Example: `<span>`, `<a>`.
- inline-block: Combines aspects of both block and inline elements, allowing you to set width and height while maintaining inline behavior.
- flex: Introduces a flexible box layout, enabling you to create responsive layouts easily. Example: `display: flex`.
- grid: Introduces a two-dimensional grid layout, offering precise control over rows and columns. Example: `display: grid`.
- none: Hides the element completely, making it invisible and not occupying space on the page.

```css
/* Setting display property */
div {
    display: block; /* Block-level element */
}

span {
    display: inline; /* Inline-level element */
}
```

Box Model

The CSS box model describes how elements are rendered as rectangular boxes with content, padding, borders, and margins. Understanding the box model is essential for precise layout control.

- Content: The inner content of the element.
- Padding: The space between the content and the element's border.
- Border: A border surrounding the padding.
- Margin: The space outside the border, affecting the element's spacing with other elements.

```css
/* Box model properties */
div {
    width: 200px;
    padding: 20px;
    border: 2px solid #333;
    margin: 10px;
}
```

Positioning

CSS provides various positioning properties to control the placement of elements on the page:

- position: Specifies the positioning method. Common values include static, relative, absolute, and fixed.

```css
/* Positioning properties */
header {
    position: relative; /* Relative positioning */
}

footer {
    position: absolute; /* Absolute positioning */
    bottom: 0; /* Align to the bottom */
    left: 0; /* Align to the left */
}
```

- float: Allows elements to float left or right within their containers, affecting the flow of surrounding content.

```css
/* Floating elements */
img {
    float: left; /* Float left */
}
```

Flexbox Layout

Flexbox is a powerful CSS layout model that simplifies the creation of flexible and responsive layouts. It allows you to distribute space within a container and align items along a single axis (either horizontally or vertically).

```css
/* Flexbox layout */
.container {
    display: flex;
    justify-content: space-between; /* Distribute space between items */
    align-items: center; /* Center items vertically */
}
```

Grid Layout

Grid layout extends the flexibility of CSS layouts by providing a two-dimensional grid system for arranging elements in rows and columns. It's highly useful for creating complex and responsive layouts.

```css
/* Grid layout */
.container {
    display: grid;
    grid-template-columns: 1fr 2fr; /* Define columns */
    grid-gap: 20px; /* Gap between grid items */
}
```

Responsive Design

Responsive web design ensures that web pages adapt to different screen sizes and devices. CSS media queries allow you to apply different styles based on screen width, height, or other factors.

```css
/* Media query for responsive design */
@media (max-width: 768px) {
    /* CSS rules for screens up to 768px wide */
}
```

CSS Positioning and Layout Resources

- CSS Flexbox Guide
- CSS Grid Guide
- MDN Web Docs on CSS Positioning
- CSS Tricks Guide on the CSS Box Model

Mastering layout and positioning in CSS is essential for creating responsive and visually appealing web designs. These techniques provide the foundation for building flexible and user-friendly web interfaces. In the following chapters, we'll explore more advanced CSS techniques and web design best practices.

Chapter 4: Advanced CSS Techniques

Section 4.1: CSS Box Model and Margins/Padding

The CSS box model is a fundamental concept in web design, defining how elements are rendered on a web page as rectangular boxes with content, padding, borders, and margins. Understanding the box model is crucial for precise layout control and spacing of elements. In this section, we'll explore the box model in depth, as well as margins and padding—two essential properties that influence the positioning and spacing of elements.

CSS Box Model Overview

The CSS box model represents an HTML element as a rectangular box with four distinct areas:

1. **Content:** The inner area of the element that holds its actual content, such as text, images, or other elements. You can control the content's size using the `width` and `height` properties.

2. **Padding:** The space between the content and the element's border. Padding is defined using the `padding` property and can be set individually for each side (e.g., `padding-top`, `padding-right`, `padding-bottom`, `padding-left`).

3. **Border:** A border surrounding the padding and content. You can specify the border's width, style, and color using properties like `border-width`, `border-style`, and `border-color`.

4. **Margin:** The space outside the element's border, influencing its positioning and spacing in relation to other elements on the page. Margins are defined using the `margin` property and can also be set individually for each side (e.g., `margin-top`, `margin-right`, `margin-bottom`, `margin-left`).

Here's an example of how the box model is represented in CSS:

```css
/* Applying the box model to an element */
.box {
    width: 200px; /* Set the width of the content area */
    height: 100px; /* Set the height of the content area */
    padding: 20px; /* Define padding for all sides */
    border: 2px solid #333; /* Specify border properties */
    margin: 10px; /* Set margins for all sides */
}
```

Box Sizing

By default, the `width` and `height` properties set the dimensions of the content area only, excluding padding, borders, and margins. This behavior can sometimes lead to unexpected layouts. To include padding and border in an element's total size, you can use the box-sizing property with the `border-box` value:

```css
/* Box sizing includes padding and border in the width and height */
.box {
    width: 200px;
    height: 100px;
    padding: 20px;
    border: 2px solid #333;
    margin: 10px;
    box-sizing: border-box;
}
```

Margins and Padding

Margins and padding are essential for controlling the spacing and layout of elements on a web page. Here's a brief overview of their properties:

- **Margins:** Margins define the space outside an element's border. They are used to create spacing between elements. You can set margins for individual sides (e.g., `margin-top`, `margin-right`) or apply values to all sides using the `margin` property.

- **Padding:** Padding is the space between an element's content and its border. It provides internal spacing within the element. Like margins, you can specify padding for individual sides (e.g., `padding-left`, `padding-bottom`) or apply values to all sides using the `padding` property.

```css
/* Setting margins and padding */
.element {
    margin: 10px; /* Apply the same margin to all sides */
    padding: 15px; /* Apply the same padding to all sides */
}
```

```css
/* Setting margins and padding for specific sides */
.box {
    margin-top: 20px;
    margin-left: 10px;
    padding-top: 30px;
    padding-right: 25px;
}
```

Margin Collapsing

Margin collapsing is a behavior where adjacent vertical margins between block-level elements collapse into a single margin. This can affect the spacing between elements and is an important concept to understand in web design.

```html
<div class="box1"></div>
<div class="box2"></div>
```

```
/* Margin collapsing example */
.box1 {
    margin-bottom: 20px;
}

.box2 {
    margin-top: 30px;
}
```

In this example, the vertical margins of `.box1` and `.box2` collapse, resulting in a total vertical space of 30px (the larger of the two margins).

Box Model Resources

- MDN Web Docs on the CSS Box Model
- CSS Tricks Guide on the CSS Box Model

Mastering the CSS box model, margins, and padding is essential for achieving precise layout control in web design. These concepts enable you to create visually appealing and well-structured web pages. In the following sections, we'll explore more advanced CSS techniques to enhance your web design skills.

Section 4.2: Flexbox and Grid Layouts

Flexbox and Grid Layout are two powerful CSS layout models that simplify the creation of complex and responsive layouts. These layout systems offer precise control over the arrangement and alignment of elements within a container. In this section, we'll explore both Flexbox and Grid Layout, explaining their key concepts and how to use them effectively.

Flexbox Layout

Flexbox, or the Flexible Box Layout, is a one-dimensional layout model designed for distributing space along a single axis—either horizontally or vertically. It's particularly useful for creating flexible and responsive layouts. Here are the fundamental concepts of Flexbox:

1. Flex Container and Items

- **Flex Container:** To create a Flexbox layout, you designate an element as the flex container by setting its `display` property to `flex` or `inline-flex`.

```
/* Creating a Flexbox container */
.container {
    display: flex;
}
```

- **Flex Items:** The child elements of a Flexbox container are referred to as flex items. They automatically become flexible and adjust their size to fit within the container.

```
<div class="container">
    <div class="item">Item 1</div>
    <div class="item">Item 2</div>
    <div class="item">Item 3</div>
</div>

/* Styling Flex items */
.item {
    flex: 1; /* All items share equal space */
}
```

2. Main and Cross Axes

In Flexbox, there are two axes: the main axis and the cross axis. The direction of the main axis is determined by the `flex-direction` property (either row or column). The cross axis is perpendicular to the main axis.

```
/* Setting the main axis direction */
.container {
    flex-direction: row; /* Main axis is horizontal */
}
```

3. Justify Content and Align Items

- **Justify Content:** The `justify-content` property controls how flex items are aligned along the main axis. Common values include `flex-start`, `flex-end`, `center`, `space-between`, and `space-around`.

```
/* Justify content along the main axis */
.container {
    justify-content: space-between; /* Items spread evenly */
}
```

- **Align Items:** The `align-items` property controls how flex items are aligned along the cross axis. Common values include `flex-start`, `flex-end`, `center`, `baseline`, and stretch.

```
/* Align items along the cross axis */
.container {
    align-items: center; /* Items centered vertically */
}
```

Grid Layout

CSS Grid Layout is a two-dimensional layout system that enables precise control over rows and columns within a grid container. It's ideal for creating grid-based designs, such as responsive web layouts. Here are the key concepts of Grid Layout:

1. Grid Container and Items

- **Grid Container:** To create a Grid Layout, designate an element as the grid container by setting its `display` property to `grid`.

```css
/* Creating a Grid Layout container */
.container {
    display: grid;
}
```

- **Grid Items:** Child elements of a Grid Layout container become grid items, and you can control their placement within the grid.

```html
<div class="container">
    <div class="item">Item 1</div>
    <div class="item">Item 2</div>
    <div class="item">Item 3</div>
</div>
```

2. Defining Grid Structure

You can define the grid's structure by specifying the number and size of rows and columns using properties like `grid-template-rows` and `grid-template-columns`.

```css
/* Defining grid rows and columns */
.container {
    grid-template-rows: 1fr 2fr; /* Two rows with relative sizes */
    grid-template-columns: 1fr 2fr; /* Two columns with relative sizes */
}
```

3. Placing Grid Items

Grid items can be placed using properties like `grid-row` and `grid-column`. You can specify the starting and ending positions for both rows and columns.

```css
/* Placing grid items */
.item1 {
    grid-row: 1 / 2; /* Starts at row 1 and ends before row 2 */
    grid-column: 1 / 2; /* Starts at column 1 and ends before column 2 */
}
```

Flexbox vs. Grid Layout

Both Flexbox and Grid Layout are valuable tools for creating web layouts, but they have different use cases:

- **Flexbox:** Best suited for one-dimensional layouts, such as navigation bars, horizontal or vertical lists, and aligning elements within a container along a single axis.

- **Grid Layout:** Ideal for two-dimensional layouts where you need precise control over rows and columns, such as responsive grids, card layouts, and complex web designs.

When used together, these layout systems can provide robust and responsive solutions for various web design challenges.

Flexbox and Grid Layout Resources
- MDN Web Docs on Flexbox
- CSS Tricks Guide on Flexbox
- MDN Web Docs on Grid Layout
- [CSS

Section 4.3: Responsive Web Design with Media Queries

Responsive web design is a crucial aspect of modern web development. It ensures that web pages adapt and look good on various devices and screen sizes, from small smartphones to large desktop monitors. Media queries are a fundamental tool for achieving responsive designs. In this section, we'll explore how to use media queries effectively to create responsive layouts.

What Are Media Queries?

Media queries are CSS techniques that allow you to apply different styles to web pages based on various factors, such as screen width, height, device orientation, and more. They enable you to target specific conditions and apply CSS rules accordingly. Media queries are essential for building responsive designs because they enable your website to respond to the user's device and viewport.

Anatomy of a Media Query

A media query consists of an @media rule followed by a condition enclosed in parentheses. If the condition is met, the CSS rules within the media query block are applied.

Here's the basic structure of a media query:

```css
@media (condition) {
    /* CSS rules for this condition */
}
```

Using Media Queries for Responsive Design

Responsive design typically involves adjusting the layout, font size, images, and other styling based on the screen size. Here's a practical example of using media queries to create a responsive design:

```css
/* Default styles for larger screens */
.header {
    font-size: 24px;
}

/* Media query for screens smaller than 768px */
@media (max-width: 768px) {
    .header {
```

```css
      font-size: 18px; /* Decrease font size for smaller screens */
   }
}

/* Media query for screens smaller than 480px */
@media (max-width: 480px) {
    .header {
        font-size: 16px; /* Further decrease font size for very small screens
*/
    }
}
```

In this example, we start with default styles for larger screens. Then, we use media queries to adjust the font size when the screen width becomes smaller.

Common Media Query Conditions

Media queries can be based on various conditions, and you can combine them to create precise responsive designs. Here are some common conditions:

- **Width and Height:** You can use `max-width` and `min-width` to target specific screen widths or heights.
- **Orientation:** Use `orientation` to target portrait or landscape orientations.
- **Device Aspect Ratio:** Target specific device aspect ratios with `aspect-ratio`.
- **Device Type:** You can use `pointer` to target devices with or without pointer capabilities (e.g., touch screens).
- **Dark Mode:** You can use `prefers-color-scheme` to adjust styles for dark or light mode.

Breakpoints and Mobile-First Design

When implementing responsive design, it's common to define breakpoints, which are specific screen widths where your design adapts. One popular approach is mobile-first design, where you start with styles for small screens and progressively enhance them for larger screens using media queries.

```css
/* Default styles for small screens (mobile-first) */
.element {
    font-size: 16px;
}

/* Media query for screens larger than 768px */
@media (min-width: 769px) {
    .element {
        font-size: 18px; /* Enhance styles for larger screens */
    }
}
```

Mobile-first design ensures that your website's core content and functionality work well on small screens and then optimizes the experience for larger screens.

Testing and Debugging

When working with media queries, it's crucial to test your responsive design on various devices and screen sizes to ensure it behaves as expected. Most modern browsers come with built-in developer tools that allow you to simulate different screen sizes and orientations for testing.

Additionally, keep an eye on the content flow and readability when adjusting font sizes and layout. Effective responsive design goes beyond just adjusting styles; it ensures a seamless user experience on all devices.

Media Query Resources

- MDN Web Docs on Media Queries
- CSS Tricks Guide on Responsive Design

Mastering media queries is essential for creating responsive web designs that provide a consistent and user-friendly experience across various devices and screen sizes. With the right use of media queries, you can ensure that your website looks and functions well for all users. In the following sections, we'll explore more advanced CSS techniques and web design best practices.

Section 4.4: CSS Transitions and Animations

CSS transitions and animations are powerful tools for adding interactivity and visual appeal to web designs. They allow you to smoothly change property values over time or create complex animations to engage users. In this section, we'll delve into CSS transitions and animations, explaining how to use them effectively.

CSS Transitions

CSS transitions enable you to smoothly change property values over a specified duration. Transitions are often used for hover effects, menu animations, and other interactive elements. Here's how to set up a basic CSS transition:

```css
/* Define the initial state */
.element {
    width: 100px;
    height: 100px;
    background-color: blue;
    transition: width 0.3s ease; /* Property to transition, duration, and
timing function */
}

/* Define the hover state */
```

```css
.element:hover {
    width: 150px; /* New property value on hover */
}
```

In this example, when you hover over the element with the class `.element`, the `width` property transitions smoothly from its initial value to the new value defined in the `:hover` state.

Transition Properties

The `transition` property accepts multiple values, allowing you to control various aspects of the transition:

- **Property to Transition:** Specifies the CSS property to transition.
- **Duration:** Defines how long the transition should take (in seconds or milliseconds).
- **Timing Function:** Specifies the timing function that determines the acceleration of the transition.
- **Delay:** Sets a delay before the transition begins (optional).

Here are some common timing functions:

- `ease`: The default timing function, which starts slow, accelerates in the middle, and slows down again.
- `linear`: Causes a constant transition speed.
- `ease-in`: Starts slow and accelerates.
- `ease-out`: Starts fast and decelerates.
- `ease-in-out`: Starts slow, accelerates, and then decelerates.

CSS Animations

While transitions are ideal for simple property changes, CSS animations offer more control and flexibility for creating complex animations. Animations involve defining keyframes and specifying how elements change between those keyframes. Here's a basic example of a CSS animation:

```css
/* Define animation keyframes */
@keyframes slide {
    0% { left: 0; }
    100% { left: 100px; }
}

/* Apply the animation to an element */
.element {
    position: relative;
    animation: slide 2s ease infinite; /* Animation name, duration, timing
function, and iteration count */
}
```

In this example, the @keyframes rule defines the animation's keyframes, and the .element class applies the animation. The element will smoothly move from left to right and repeat infinitely.

Animation Properties

CSS animations use several properties to control their behavior:

- **animation-name:** Specifies the name of the keyframes animation.
- **animation-duration:** Sets the animation's duration.
- **animation-timing-function:** Defines the timing function for the animation.
- **animation-delay:** Specifies the delay before the animation starts (optional).
- **animation-iteration-count:** Determines how many times the animation repeats.
- **animation-direction:** Specifies whether the animation plays forwards, backward, or alternates.
- **animation-fill-mode:** Sets the style applied to the element before and after the animation.
- **animation-play-state:** Controls whether the animation is running or paused.

Choosing Between Transitions and Animations

Transitions and animations serve different purposes:

- **Transitions:** Ideal for simple, single-property changes triggered by user interactions like hover effects or button clicks.

- **Animations:** More suitable for complex and multi-property animations where you need precise control over the animation sequence.

When deciding between transitions and animations, consider the complexity of your design and the desired user experience.

Animation Libraries

For more advanced animations, you can use CSS animation libraries like GreenSock Animation Platform (GSAP) or Animate.css. These libraries provide pre-built animations and tools for creating stunning web animations.

Resources

- MDN Web Docs on CSS Transitions
- MDN Web Docs on CSS Animations
- GreenSock Animation Platform (GSAP)

CSS transitions and animations are essential tools for enhancing user interactions and creating visually appealing web designs. By mastering these techniques, you can add a dynamic and engaging dimension to your web projects. In the following sections, we'll explore more advanced CSS techniques and web design best practices.

Section 4.5: CSS Preprocessors like SASS or LESS

CSS preprocessors like SASS (Syntactically Awesome Stylesheets) and LESS (Leaner CSS) are tools that extend the capabilities of traditional CSS. They introduce features like variables, nesting, mixins, and functions, making CSS code more maintainable, modular, and efficient. In this section, we'll explore the benefits of using CSS preprocessors and how to get started with SASS and LESS.

Why Use CSS Preprocessors?

CSS preprocessors offer several advantages for web developers and designers:

1. **Variables:** Preprocessors allow you to define and reuse variables for colors, fonts, sizes, and other CSS properties. This simplifies maintenance and ensures consistency throughout your stylesheet.

2. **Nesting:** You can nest CSS selectors within one another, mirroring the structure of your HTML. This makes your styles more readable and reduces redundancy.

3. **Mixins:** Mixins are reusable blocks of CSS that can include multiple properties and values. They help you avoid repetitive code and maintain consistency.

4. **Functions:** Preprocessors support functions that can manipulate values or perform calculations, offering dynamic styling capabilities.

5. **Modularity:** Preprocessors encourage modularity by breaking down stylesheets into smaller files or components, making it easier to manage and scale projects.

Getting Started with SASS

SASS is one of the most popular CSS preprocessors. To start using SASS, follow these steps:

1. **Installation:** You can install SASS globally using Node.js and npm (Node Package Manager):

```
npm install -g sass
```

2. **Compile SASS to CSS:** Create a `.scss` file (SASS file) and compile it to CSS using the `sass` command-line tool:

```
sass input.scss output.css
```

3. **Basic Syntax:** Here's a simple example of SASS syntax:

```scss
// Define a variable
$primary-color: #3498db;

// Use the variable
.button {
```

```
        background-color: $primary-color;
    }
```

4. **Nesting:** SASS allows you to nest selectors:

```
.navigation {
    ul {
        list-style: none;
        li {
            display: inline-block;
        }
    }
}
```

5. **Mixins:** Define and use mixins for reusable styles:

```
@mixin border-radius($radius) {
    border-radius: $radius;
}

.element {
    @include border-radius(5px);
}
```

Getting Started with LESS

LESS is another popular CSS preprocessor. To start using LESS, follow these steps:

1. **Installation:** You can install LESS globally using npm:

```
npm install -g less
```

2. **Compile LESS to CSS:** Create a .less file (LESS file) and compile it to CSS using the lessc command-line tool:

```
lessc input.less output.css
```

3. **Basic Syntax:** Here's a simple example of LESS syntax:

```
// Define a variable
@primary-color: #3498db;

// Use the variable
.button {
    background-color: @primary-color;
}
```

4. **Nesting:** LESS allows you to nest selectors:

```
.navigation {
    ul {
```

```
            list-style: none;
            li {
                display: inline-block;
            }
        }
```

5. **Mixins:** Define and use mixins for reusable styles:

```
.border-radius(@radius) {
    border-radius: @radius;
}

.element {
    .border-radius(5px);
}
```

Integrating with Build Tools

Both SASS and LESS can be integrated into your build process. You can use task runners like Gulp or Webpack to automatically compile your preprocessor files into CSS, minify the output, and handle other optimization tasks.

Preprocessor Resources
- SASS Official Website
- LESS Official Website
- Comparing SASS and LESS

CSS preprocessors offer powerful features that simplify and improve the development process. By incorporating variables, nesting, mixins, and functions, you can write cleaner, more maintainable CSS code. These preprocessors are widely adopted in the web development community and can boost your productivity as a web designer or developer. In the following chapters, we'll explore additional web design best practices and advanced techniques to enhance your skills further.

Chapter 5: JavaScript Basics

Section 5.1: Introduction to JavaScript

JavaScript is a versatile and essential programming language for web development. It allows you to add interactivity, manipulate the Document Object Model (DOM), and perform various tasks on web pages. In this section, we'll provide an introduction to JavaScript, covering its basic concepts and how to get started with coding in this language.

What Is JavaScript?

JavaScript is a high-level, interpreted scripting language that runs in web browsers. It was created to make web pages more dynamic by allowing developers to add logic and behavior to HTML and CSS. JavaScript can be used for a wide range of tasks, including form validation, interactive animations, and fetching data from servers.

JavaScript in Web Development

JavaScript plays a crucial role in web development for the following reasons:

1. **Interactivity:** JavaScript enables you to create interactive elements on web pages, such as buttons, sliders, and forms. You can define how these elements respond to user actions like clicks and input.

2. **Dynamic Content:** With JavaScript, you can manipulate the DOM to add, remove, or modify elements and content dynamically. This is essential for single-page applications and real-time updates.

3. **Client-Side Validation:** You can use JavaScript to validate user input on the client side, providing immediate feedback to users and reducing the load on the server.

4. **Asynchronous Operations:** JavaScript supports asynchronous programming, allowing you to make requests to servers and perform tasks without blocking the user interface.

5. **Browser Compatibility:** It's a universal language supported by all modern web browsers, making it a reliable choice for client-side scripting.

How to Include JavaScript in HTML

You can include JavaScript code in an HTML document using the `<script>` element. There are two main ways to do this:

1. **Inline JavaScript:** You can include JavaScript code directly within your HTML document by placing it inside `<script>` tags within the `<body>` or `<head>` section.

```
<!DOCTYPE html>
<html>
```

```
<head>
    <title>My Web Page</title>
    <script>
        // Your JavaScript code here
        alert('Hello, World!');
    </script>
</head>
<body>
    <!-- Content of your web page -->
</body>
</html>
```

Placing scripts in the <head> section is common for scripts that need to run before the page content is loaded.

2. **External JavaScript:** For larger scripts or better code organization, you can create separate JavaScript files with a .js extension and link them in your HTML using the <script> tag's src attribute.

```
<!DOCTYPE html>
<html>
<head>
    <title>My Web Page</title>
</head>
<body>
    <!-- Content of your web page -->
    <script src="script.js"></script>
</body>
</html>
```

In this example, script.js contains your JavaScript code.

Basic JavaScript Syntax

JavaScript uses a C-style syntax with statements terminated by semicolons. Here's a simple example of JavaScript code that displays a message in a web browser's console:

```
// This is a single-line comment
/* This is a
   multi-line comment */
console.log('Hello, World!');
```

Key points to note in this code:

- Comments are used to document code. Single-line comments start with //, and multi-line comments are enclosed between /* and */.
- The console.log() function is used to output messages to the browser's developer console. It's a helpful tool for debugging.

Variables and Data Types

JavaScript variables are used to store data values. You can declare variables using the var, let, or const keywords. Here's an example:

```
var name = 'John'; // Declaring a variable and assigning a string value
let age = 30; // Declaring a variable with let and assigning a number
const PI = 3.14159; // Declaring a constant variable
```

JavaScript supports various data types, including strings, numbers, booleans, arrays, objects, and more. Variables can change their data type dynamically during runtime.

Operators and Expressions

JavaScript provides operators for performing operations on data values. Common operators include arithmetic operators (+, -, *, /), comparison operators (==, !=, >, <), and logical operators (&&, ||, !), among others.

Expressions in JavaScript are combinations of values and operators that can be evaluated to produce a result. For example:

```
var x = 5;
var y = 10;
var result = x + y; // The expression calculates the sum of x and y
```

Control Structures

Control structures in JavaScript allow you to make decisions and control the flow of your code. Common control structures include:

- **Conditional Statements:** if, else if, and else statements for executing code conditionally.
- **Loops:** for, while, and do...while loops for repeating code.
- **Switch Statement:** For handling multiple conditions in a more structured way.

Here's an example of an if statement:

```
var age = 18;

if (age >= 18) {
    console.log('You are an adult.');
} else {
    console.log('You are a minor.');
}
```

Functions and Scope

Functions in JavaScript are reusable blocks of code that can take input (parameters) and return output. They allow you to encapsulate logic and reuse it throughout your code.

```
// Defining a function
function greet(name) {
    return 'Hello, ' + name + '!';
}

// Calling the function
var message = greet('Alice');
console.log(message); // Output: "Hello, Alice!"
```

JavaScript also has function scope and block scope. Variables declared with var have function scope, while variables declared with let and const have block scope.

JavaScript Resources

To continue learning JavaScript, refer to the following resources:

- MDN Web Docs - JavaScript
- JavaScript.info
- Codecademy JavaScript Course

JavaScript is a fundamental language for web development, and mastering its basics is essential for building interactive and dynamic web applications. In the upcoming sections, we'll delve deeper into JavaScript, covering more advanced topics and techniques.

Section 5.2: Variables and Data Types in JavaScript

Variables and data types are fundamental concepts in JavaScript. They allow you to store and manipulate data within your programs. In this section, we'll explore how to work with variables and the various data types available in JavaScript.

Declaring Variables

In JavaScript, you can declare variables using the var, let, or const keywords. The choice of keyword affects the variable's scope and mutability:

- **var** (Function-Scoped): Variables declared with var are function-scoped, meaning they are visible within the function where they are declared or, if declared outside a function, they become global variables.

- **let** and **const** (Block-Scoped): Variables declared with let and const are block-scoped, which means they are confined to the block (within curly braces) where they are defined. let allows reassignment, while const is for variables that should not be reassigned.

Here are examples of variable declarations:

```
var name = 'John'; // Declaring a variable using var
let age = 30; // Declaring a variable using let
const PI = 3.14159; // Declaring a constant variable using const
```

Data Types

JavaScript supports several data types, including:

1. **Primitive Data Types:**
   - **String:** Represents text. Example: "Hello, World!".
   - **Number:** Represents numeric values, including integers and floats. Example: 42 or 3.14.
   - **Boolean:** Represents true or false values, often used for conditional statements.
   - **Undefined:** Represents a variable that has been declared but not assigned a value.
   - **Null:** Represents an intentional absence of any object value.
2. **Reference Data Types:**
   - **Object:** Represents a collection of key-value pairs. Objects are versatile and can represent complex data structures.
   - **Array:** Represents an ordered list of values. Arrays are a specific type of object.
   - **Function:** A special type of object that can be invoked (called) to perform a task or return a value.

Type Coercion

JavaScript performs type coercion, which means it can automatically convert values from one data type to another when needed. This behavior can lead to unexpected results if not understood correctly. For example:

```
var num = 5;
var str = '10';
var result = num + str; // JavaScript coerces num to a string and performs
string concatenation
console.log(result); // Output: "510"
```

Variable Naming Rules

When naming variables in JavaScript, follow these rules:

- Variable names are case-sensitive (myVar is different from myvar).
- Names can consist of letters, digits, underscores, and dollar signs.
- Names must begin with a letter, underscore, or dollar sign.
- Variable names should be descriptive and follow a meaningful naming convention (e.g., firstName, totalAmount, isLogged).

Hoisting

JavaScript has a behavior called "hoisting," which means variable and function declarations are moved to the top of their containing scope during compilation. However, only the declarations are hoisted, not their initializations. Here's an example:

```
console.log(x); // Output: undefined
var x = 10;
```

In this code, the variable x is hoisted to the top, but its value is undefined until it's explicitly assigned the value 10.

Conclusion

Variables and data types are essential building blocks of JavaScript programming. Understanding how to declare variables, work with different data types, and handle type coercion is fundamental to writing effective JavaScript code. In the following sections, we'll explore more advanced JavaScript topics and techniques to enhance your programming skills.

Section 5.3: Operators and Expressions in JavaScript

Operators and expressions in JavaScript allow you to perform various operations on data, make comparisons, and evaluate conditions. Understanding these concepts is crucial for writing dynamic and interactive scripts. In this section, we'll explore the different types of operators and how to use them in JavaScript.

Arithmetic Operators

JavaScript provides arithmetic operators for performing basic mathematical operations:

- **Addition (+):** Adds two values together.
- **Subtraction (-):** Subtracts the right operand from the left operand.
- **Multiplication (*):** Multiplies two values.
- **Division (/):** Divides the left operand by the right operand.
- **Modulus (%):** Returns the remainder when the left operand is divided by the right operand.

Here are some examples of arithmetic operations:

```
var num1 = 10;
var num2 = 5;

var sum = num1 + num2; // Addition
var difference = num1 - num2; // Subtraction
var product = num1 * num2; // Multiplication
var quotient = num1 / num2; // Division
var remainder = num1 % num2; // Modulus
```

```
console.log(sum, difference, product, quotient, remainder);
```

Comparison Operators

Comparison operators are used to compare two values and return a Boolean result (true or false). Common comparison operators include:

- **Equal to (==):** Checks if two values are equal.
- **Not equal to (!=):** Checks if two values are not equal.
- **Greater than (>):** Checks if the left operand is greater than the right operand.
- **Less than (<):** Checks if the left operand is less than the right operand.
- **Greater than or equal to (>=):** Checks if the left operand is greater than or equal to the right operand.
- **Less than or equal to (<=):** Checks if the left operand is less than or equal to the right operand.

Here's how comparison operators are used:

```
var x = 5;
var y = 10;

var isEqual = x == y; // Equal to
var isNotEqual = x != y; // Not equal to
var isGreaterThan = x > y; // Greater than
var isLessThan = x < y; // Less than
var isGreaterOrEqual = x >= y; // Greater than or equal to
var isLessOrEqual = x <= y; // Less than or equal to

console.log(isEqual, isNotEqual, isGreaterThan, isLessThan, isGreaterOrEqual,
isLessOrEqual);
```

Logical Operators

Logical operators allow you to perform logical operations on Boolean values. JavaScript has three primary logical operators:

- **Logical AND (&&):** Returns true if both operands are true.
- **Logical OR (||):** Returns true if at least one operand is true.
- **Logical NOT (!):** Inverts the value of the operand (if true, becomes false, and vice versa).

Here's how logical operators work:

```
var isTrue = true;
var isFalse = false;

var andResult = isTrue && isFalse; // Logical AND
var orResult = isTrue || isFalse; // Logical OR
```

```
var notResult = !isTrue; // Logical NOT

console.log(andResult, orResult, notResult);
```

Conditional (Ternary) Operator

The conditional operator (? :) is a shorthand way to write simple conditional statements. It allows you to specify a condition and two possible outcomes. If the condition is true, the first expression is evaluated; otherwise, the second expression is evaluated.

Here's an example:

```
var age = 18;
var canVote = age >= 18 ? 'Yes' : 'No';

console.log('Can vote:', canVote);
```

In this code, if age is greater than or equal to 18, canVote will be assigned the value 'Yes'; otherwise, it will be assigned 'No'.

Operator Precedence

JavaScript follows a specific order of precedence when evaluating expressions with multiple operators. You can use parentheses to control the order of evaluation. For example, () has the highest precedence, followed by arithmetic, comparison, logical, and finally, the conditional operator.

Here's an example that demonstrates operator precedence:

```
var result = 2 * (3 + 4) > 10 && !(5 < 2);
console.log(result); // Output: true
```

Conclusion

Operators and expressions are fundamental to JavaScript programming. They enable you to perform calculations, make decisions, and control the flow of your code. Understanding how to use arithmetic, comparison, logical operators, and the conditional operator is essential for writing efficient and effective JavaScript programs. In the upcoming sections, we'll explore more advanced JavaScript concepts and techniques to further enhance your coding skills.

Section 5.4: Control Structures in JavaScript

Control structures in JavaScript are essential for controlling the flow of your code, making decisions, and repeating tasks. They allow you to create dynamic and interactive programs. In this section, we'll explore different control structures, including conditional statements and loops.

Conditional Statements

Conditional statements allow you to execute different code blocks based on whether a condition is true or false. JavaScript provides if, else if, and else statements for this purpose.

if Statement

The if statement evaluates a condition, and if the condition is true, it executes a specified block of code. If the condition is false, the code block is skipped.

```javascript
var age = 18;

if (age >= 18) {
    console.log('You are an adult.');
}
```

else Statement

The else statement is used in conjunction with if to specify a code block that should be executed when the condition in the if statement is false.

```javascript
var age = 16;

if (age >= 18) {
    console.log('You are an adult.');
} else {
    console.log('You are a minor.');
}
```

else if Statement

The else if statement allows you to specify multiple conditions to test. It is used when you have multiple possible outcomes.

```javascript
var time = 14;

if (time < 12) {
    console.log('Good morning!');
} else if (time < 18) {
    console.log('Good afternoon!');
} else {
    console.log('Good evening!');
}
```

Loops

Loops in JavaScript allow you to execute a block of code repeatedly as long as a condition is true. There are different types of loops, including for, while, and do...while.

for Loop

The `for` loop is used when you know in advance how many times you want to execute a block of code. It consists of an initialization, a condition, and an increment or decrement statement.

```
for (var i = 0; i < 5; i++) {
    console.log('Iteration ' + i);
}
```

while Loop

The `while` loop repeatedly executes a block of code as long as a specified condition is true.

```
var count = 0;

while (count < 5) {
    console.log('Count: ' + count);
    count++;
}
```

do...while Loop

The `do...while` loop is similar to the `while` loop, but it ensures that the code block is executed at least once before checking the condition.

```
var num = 0;

do {
    console.log('Number: ' + num);
    num++;
} while (num < 5);
```

Switch Statement

The `switch` statement is used when you have multiple possible conditions to test. It provides a more efficient way to handle multiple conditions compared to using multiple `if` statements.

```
var day = 'Monday';

switch (day) {
    case 'Monday':
        console.log('It\'s the start of the week.');
        break;
    case 'Friday':
        console.log('TGIF! It\'s Friday.');
        break;
    default:
        console.log('It\'s a regular day.');
}
```

Control Statements

Control statements like `break` and `continue` are used within loops to control their behavior. `break` is used to exit a loop prematurely, while `continue` is used to skip the current iteration and continue to the next.

```javascript
for (var i = 0; i < 5; i++) {
    if (i === 3) {
        break; // Exit the loop when i is 3
    }
    console.log('Iteration ' + i);
}
```

Conclusion

Control structures are vital for creating interactive and dynamic JavaScript programs. They allow you to make decisions, repeat tasks, and handle different scenarios in your code. Understanding how to use conditional statements, loops, and control statements is essential for effective programming in JavaScript. In the following sections, we'll delve into more advanced topics and techniques to enhance your JavaScript skills.

Section 5.5: Functions and Scope in JavaScript

Functions are a fundamental concept in JavaScript that allow you to encapsulate reusable blocks of code. They play a crucial role in structuring your programs and promoting code reusability. In this section, we'll explore functions, their syntax, and how variable scope works in JavaScript.

Function Declaration

A function in JavaScript can be declared using the `function` keyword followed by a name, a list of parameters enclosed in parentheses, and a code block enclosed in curly braces.

```javascript
function greet(name) {
    console.log('Hello, ' + name + '!');
}

// Calling the function
greet('John'); // Output: Hello, John!
```

In this example, `greet` is a function that takes a `name` parameter and logs a greeting message to the console.

Function Expression

You can also define functions as expressions. In this case, the function is assigned to a variable.

```
var greet = function(name) {
    console.log('Hello, ' + name + '!');
};

// Calling the function
greet('Alice'); // Output: Hello, Alice!
```

Arrow Functions

Arrow functions provide a concise way to define functions, especially for one-liner functions. They use the => syntax.

```
var greet = (name) => console.log('Hello, ' + name + '!');

// Calling the function
greet('Bob'); // Output: Hello, Bob!
```

Function Scope

Variables declared within a function are local to that function, meaning they are only accessible within the function's code block. This concept is known as "function scope."

```
function exampleScope() {
    var localVar = 'I am a local variable';
    console.log(localVar);
}

exampleScope(); // Output: I am a local variable

// Attempting to access localVar outside the function will result in an error
console.log(localVar); // Error: localVar is not defined
```

Global Scope

Variables declared outside of any function are considered "global" and can be accessed from anywhere in the script.

```
var globalVar = 'I am a global variable';

function accessGlobal() {
    console.log(globalVar);
}

accessGlobal(); // Output: I am a global variable
console.log(globalVar); // Output: I am a global variable
```

However, it's important to use global variables judiciously to avoid unintended side effects and naming conflicts.

Functions can accept parameters, which are placeholders for values passed when the function is called. They can also return values using the return statement.

```javascript
function add(a, b) {
    return a + b;
}

var result = add(5, 3);
console.log(result); // Output: 8
```

Conclusion

Functions are essential building blocks of JavaScript programs. They allow you to encapsulate logic, promote code reusability, and maintain clean and organized code. Understanding how to declare and use functions, as well as the concept of scope, is crucial for writing effective JavaScript code. In the next sections, we'll dive into more advanced JavaScript topics and techniques to enhance your programming skills.

Chapter 6: Document Object Model (DOM)

Section 6.1: Understanding the DOM

The Document Object Model, commonly referred to as the DOM, is a programming interface for web documents. It represents the structure of an HTML document as a tree-like structure, where each node in the tree corresponds to a part of the document, such as elements, attributes, and text. Understanding the DOM is crucial for web developers because it allows them to access, manipulate, and dynamically change the content and structure of a web page using JavaScript.

What Is the DOM?

The DOM is essentially an API (Application Programming Interface) for HTML and XML documents. It provides a structured way to interact with web pages programmatically. When a web browser loads an HTML document, it parses the HTML code and creates a hierarchical representation of the document in memory, which is the DOM. This representation allows developers to:

1. **Access Elements:** You can access elements (e.g., paragraphs, headings, images) within a web page using JavaScript. This enables you to retrieve and modify the content and attributes of these elements.

2. **Modify Content:** You can dynamically change the content of a web page without requiring a page refresh. For example, you can update the text of a paragraph, add new elements, or remove existing ones.

3. **Respond to Events:** You can add event listeners to DOM elements to handle user interactions like clicks, mouse movements, and keyboard input.

4. **Create Interactive Web Pages:** By manipulating the DOM, you can create interactive and dynamic web pages that respond to user actions.

DOM Tree Structure

The DOM is structured as a tree, with the HTML document's root at the top. Each element in the document, including the HTML element, is represented as a node in the tree. The relationships between elements are represented by parent-child relationships in the tree structure.

Here's a simplified example of a DOM tree for an HTML document:

```
<!DOCTYPE html>
<html>
  <head>
    <title>Sample Page</title>
  </head>
  <body>
    <h1>Welcome to the DOM</h1>
    <p>This is a sample paragraph.</p>
  </body>
</html>
```

In this example, the DOM tree structure would look something like this:

```
- Document (root)
  - html
    - head
      - title
        - Text: Sample Page
    - body
      - h1
        - Text: Welcome to the DOM
      - p
        - Text: This is a sample paragraph.
```

Browser Compatibility

One important consideration when working with the DOM is browser compatibility. Different web browsers may implement the DOM API slightly differently. Therefore, developers often use libraries like jQuery or modern JavaScript frameworks to abstract away some of the cross-browser inconsistencies and provide a unified interface for DOM manipulation.

Understanding the DOM is a fundamental skill for web developers, as it forms the basis for creating dynamic and interactive web applications. In the following sections, we will delve deeper into how to access and manipulate the DOM using JavaScript, along with practical examples of DOM manipulation techniques.

Section 6.2: Accessing and Manipulating DOM Elements

In the Document Object Model (DOM), elements in an HTML document are represented as nodes in a tree-like structure. To interact with and manipulate these elements, you need to know how to access them using JavaScript. In this section, we'll explore various methods for accessing and manipulating DOM elements.

Accessing DOM Elements

By ID

One common way to access a specific DOM element is by its unique id attribute. You can use the getElementById method to retrieve the element with a specified ID.

```
// HTML element with id="myElement"
var element = document.getElementById('myElement');

// You can now work with "element"
element.innerHTML = 'Hello, DOM!';
```

By Tag Name

To select multiple elements with the same tag name, you can use the getElementsByTagName method. This returns an array-like collection of elements.

```
// Select all <p> elements on the page
var paragraphs = document.getElementsByTagName('p');

// Loop through the collection of <p> elements
for (var i = 0; i < paragraphs.length; i++) {
    paragraphs[i].style.color = 'blue';
}
```

By Class Name

You can select elements with a specific class using the getElementsByClassName method.

```
// Select all elements with class "highlight"
var highlightedElements = document.getElementsByClassName('highlight');

// Manipulate the selected elements
for (var i = 0; i < highlightedElements.length; i++) {
    highlightedElements[i].style.backgroundColor = 'yellow';
}
```

Query Selector

The querySelector method allows you to select elements using CSS selectors. It returns the first matching element it finds.

```
// Select the first <p> element with class "important"
var importantParagraph = document.querySelector('p.important');

// Modify the selected element
importantParagraph.textContent = 'This is vital!';
```

Query Selector All

To select all elements that match a CSS selector, you can use `querySelectorAll`. It returns a NodeList containing all matching elements.

```
// Select all <a> elements with a "target" attribute
var linksWithTarget = document.querySelectorAll('a[target]');

// Loop through the NodeList
linksWithTarget.forEach(function(link) {
    link.setAttribute('rel', 'noopener');
});
```

Manipulating DOM Elements

Once you've selected DOM elements, you can manipulate them in various ways:

Changing Content

You can modify the content of elements by updating their `textContent` or `innerHTML` properties.

```
var element = document.getElementById('myElement');
element.textContent = 'New text content';
element.innerHTML = '<strong>Bold text</strong>';
```

Modifying Attributes

To change element attributes like `src`, `href`, or `class`, you can use the `setAttribute` method.

```
var image = document.getElementById('myImage');
image.setAttribute('src', 'new-image.jpg');

var link = document.querySelector('a');
link.setAttribute('href', 'https://example.com');
```

Adding and Removing Classes

You can add or remove CSS classes to/from elements using the `classList` property.

```
var element = document.getElementById('myElement');
element.classList.add('highlight'); // Add the "highlight" class
element.classList.remove('inactive'); // Remove the "inactive" class
```

To create new DOM elements, you can use the `createElement` method.

```
var newDiv = document.createElement('div');
newDiv.textContent = 'Newly created div';
document.body.appendChild(newDiv); // Append the new element to the body
```

Removing Elements

To remove an element from the DOM, you can use the `remove` method.

```
var elementToRemove = document.getElementById('toBeRemoved');
elementToRemove.remove();
```

These are some fundamental techniques for accessing and manipulating DOM elements using JavaScript. Understanding these methods is essential for building dynamic and interactive web applications. In the next section, we'll explore event handling and how to respond to user interactions with the DOM.

Section 6.3: Event Handling and Event Listeners

Event handling is a crucial aspect of web development, as it allows web pages to respond to user interactions like clicks, mouse movements, and keyboard input. In the Document Object Model (DOM), you can use event listeners to attach functions or scripts to specific events triggered by DOM elements. This section explores event handling in the context of web development.

Understanding Events

An event is a specific occurrence that takes place within a web page, such as a user clicking a button, moving the mouse, or pressing a key. DOM elements can "listen" for these events and execute functions in response. Common events include:

- **Click:** Triggered when the user clicks an element.
- **Mouse Over/Out:** Fired when the mouse pointer enters or leaves an element.
- **Key Press:** Occurs when a key on the keyboard is pressed.
- **Submit:** Fired when a form is submitted.
- **Load:** Triggered when a page or an external resource finishes loading.

Event Listeners

To respond to events, you can attach event listeners to DOM elements. An event listener is a JavaScript function that "listens" for a specific event on a particular element and executes a predefined action when the event occurs.

Here's an example of attaching a click event listener to a button element:

```
// Select the button element by its ID
var button = document.getElementById('myButton');

// Add a click event listener
button.addEventListener('click', function() {
    alert('Button clicked!');
});
```

In this example, when the button with the ID "myButton" is clicked, the function inside the addEventListener call will be executed, displaying an alert.

Event Object

When an event occurs, an event object is automatically created and passed to the event handler function. This object contains information about the event, such as the type of event, the target element, and more. You can access this information to make decisions based on the event.

```
var button = document.getElementById('myButton');

button.addEventListener('click', function(event) {
    // Access event properties
    console.log('Event type:', event.type);
    console.log('Target element:', event.target);
});
```

Removing Event Listeners

You can also remove event listeners when they are no longer needed. This can help prevent memory leaks in your web application.

```
function handleClick() {
    alert('Button clicked!');
}

var button = document.getElementById('myButton');

// Add the event listener
button.addEventListener('click', handleClick);

// Remove the event listener
button.removeEventListener('click', handleClick);
```

Event Propagation

In the DOM, events can propagate through the tree structure of elements. There are two phases of event propagation: capturing and bubbling. Event listeners can be set to respond during the capturing phase, the bubbling phase, or both.

- **Capturing Phase:** The event starts from the root of the tree and moves down to the target element.
- **Bubbling Phase:** The event starts from the target element and moves up to the root.

You can control the phase during which an event listener responds by passing an options object as the third parameter to addEventListener.

```
var button = document.getElementById('myButton');

button.addEventListener('click', function() {
    alert('Button clicked during bubbling phase');
}, false); // "false" means bubbling phase

button.addEventListener('click', function() {
    alert('Button clicked during capturing phase');
}, true); // "true" means capturing phase
```

Understanding event propagation is important when dealing with complex DOM structures or when you want to control how events are handled.

Event Delegation

Event delegation is a technique where you attach a single event listener to a common ancestor of multiple elements, rather than attaching listeners to each individual element. This is particularly useful when you have a list of items and want to respond to clicks on any of them without adding a separate listener to each item.

```
<ul id="myList">
    <li>Item 1</li>
    <li>Item 2</li>
    <li>Item 3</li>
</ul>

<script>
    var list = document.getElementById('myList');

    list.addEventListener('click', function(event) {
        if (event.target.tagName === 'LI') {
            alert('Clicked on ' + event.target.textContent);
        }
    });
</script>
```

In this example, a single click event listener is added to the ul element, and the listener checks which li element was clicked by inspecting the event.target property.

Event handling is a fundamental concept for building interactive and responsive web applications. By mastering event listeners, you can create web pages that respond to user actions effectively. In the next section, we'll explore how to modify HTML and CSS using JavaScript to dynamically update web pages.

Section 6.4: Modifying HTML and CSS with JavaScript

In web development, you often need to change the content, structure, or style of a web page dynamically based on user interactions or other events. JavaScript provides powerful tools for modifying both the HTML and CSS of a web page. This section explores how to use JavaScript to update HTML content and manipulate CSS styles effectively.

Modifying HTML Content

JavaScript allows you to change the content of HTML elements dynamically. Common ways to modify HTML content include:

InnerHTML

The innerHTML property allows you to set or get the HTML content within an element. You can use it to replace the content of an element with new HTML.

```
var element = document.getElementById('myElement');

// Replace the content of the element
element.innerHTML = '<strong>New content</strong>';
```

TextContent

The textContent property sets or gets the text content of an element, excluding any HTML tags. It's useful for updating text without interpreting HTML.

```
var paragraph = document.getElementById('myParagraph');

// Update the text content
paragraph.textContent = 'Updated text';
```

CreateElement

You can create new HTML elements and append them to the DOM using the createElement and appendChild methods. This is particularly useful for adding dynamic content.

```
var newDiv = document.createElement('div');
newDiv.textContent = 'Newly created div';

// Append the new element to an existing element
document.body.appendChild(newDiv);
```

RemoveChild

To remove an element from the DOM, you can use the removeChild method on its parent node.

```
var elementToRemove = document.getElementById('toBeRemoved');
var parent = elementToRemove.parentNode;

// Remove the element
parent.removeChild(elementToRemove);
```

Modifying CSS Styles

JavaScript can also be used to modify CSS styles, enabling dynamic styling of web pages. Here are some techniques for changing CSS styles using JavaScript:

Style Property

The `style` property of an element allows you to access and modify its inline CSS styles directly.

```
var element = document.getElementById('myElement');

// Change the background color
element.style.backgroundColor = 'blue';

// Modify the font size
element.style.fontSize = '16px';
```

ClassList

You can add, remove, or toggle CSS classes using the `classList` property. This is useful for applying predefined styles to elements.

```
var element = document.getElementById('myElement');

// Add a CSS class
element.classList.add('highlight');

// Remove a CSS class
element.classList.remove('inactive');

// Toggle a CSS class
element.classList.toggle('active');
```

SetAttribute

The `setAttribute` method can be used to set or update element attributes, including inline style attributes.

```
var element = document.getElementById('myElement');

// Set an inline style attribute
element.setAttribute('style', 'color: red; font-size: 18px;');
```

Practical Examples

Combining HTML and CSS modification with event handling allows you to create interactive web pages. For example, you can change the appearance of an element when the user clicks a button:

```html
<button id="myButton">Change Color</button>
<div id="myDiv">This is a div element.</div>

<script>
    var button = document.getElementById('myButton');
    var div = document.getElementById('myDiv');

    button.addEventListener('click', function() {
        // Change the background color of the div
        div.style.backgroundColor = 'green';
    });
</script>
```

In this example, clicking the button changes the background color of the div element to green. This demonstrates how JavaScript can be used to create responsive and interactive web pages.

Understanding how to modify HTML and CSS with JavaScript is essential for building dynamic web applications. These techniques allow you to create user-friendly and visually appealing websites that respond to user input and events.

Section 6.5: DOM Traversal and Manipulation Techniques

When working with JavaScript in web development, you often need to navigate and manipulate the Document Object Model (DOM) efficiently. DOM traversal and manipulation are essential skills for creating dynamic web pages. In this section, we'll explore techniques for traversing and manipulating the DOM using JavaScript.

Traversing the DOM

Traversing the DOM means moving through the hierarchy of elements to access specific elements or their properties. Common methods for DOM traversal include:

getElementById

The getElementById method allows you to directly access an element by its unique ID.

```javascript
var element = document.getElementById('myElement');
```

querySelector and querySelectorAll

These methods enable you to select elements using CSS-like selectors. querySelector returns the first matching element, while querySelectorAll returns a collection of all matching elements.

```
var firstDiv = document.querySelector('div'); // Selects the first <div>
element
var allParagraphs = document.querySelectorAll('p'); // Selects all <p>
elements
```

Parent, Child, and Sibling Relationships

You can navigate the DOM using parent, child, and sibling relationships:

- parentNode: Access the parent node of an element.
- childNodes: Get a collection of all child nodes.
- firstChild and lastChild: Access the first and last child nodes.
- nextSibling and previousSibling: Access adjacent sibling nodes.

```
var parentElement = element.parentNode;
var firstChildElement = parentElement.firstChild;
var nextSiblingElement = element.nextSibling;
```

getElementsByTagName and getElementsByClassName

These methods allow you to select elements based on their tag names or class names.

```
var allLinks = document.getElementsByTagName('a'); // Selects all <a>
elements
var elementsWithClass = document.getElementsByClassName('myClass'); //
Selects elements with the class "myClass"
```

Modifying the DOM

Once you've selected elements, you can manipulate them in various ways:

Changing Element Attributes

You can modify attributes of an element using properties like innerHTML, textContent, and setAttribute.

```
element.innerHTML = 'New content';
element.textContent = 'Text content';
element.setAttribute('class', 'newClass');
```

Creating and Appending Elements

You can create new elements and append them to the DOM using createElement and appendChild.

```
var newElement = document.createElement('div');
newElement.textContent = 'Newly created element';
parentElement.appendChild(newElement);
```

Removing Elements

To remove an element, you can use the `remove` method or its parent's `removeChild` method.

```
elementToRemove.remove(); // Modern method
parentElement.removeChild(elementToRemove); // Traditional method
```

Modifying Element Styles

You can change the CSS styles of elements using the `style` property.

```
element.style.color = 'red';
element.style.backgroundColor = 'yellow';
```

Adding and Removing Classes

Manipulating classes with the `classList` property is useful for adding, removing, or toggling CSS classes.

```
element.classList.add('newClass');
element.classList.remove('oldClass');
element.classList.toggle('active');
```

Practical Use Cases

DOM traversal and manipulation techniques are commonly used to create dynamic web pages and enhance user interactions. For example, you can build interactive forms that validate user input, update content based on user actions, or implement responsive navigation menus. Understanding these techniques is essential for modern web development and creating engaging user experiences.

Chapter 7: Interactive Web Pages with JavaScript

Section 7.1: Creating Dynamic Content

In web development, creating dynamic content is a fundamental aspect of building interactive and user-friendly web pages. JavaScript plays a pivotal role in achieving this by allowing you to manipulate the DOM and update the content of your web page dynamically in response to user interactions or other events.

The Need for Dynamic Content

Static web pages have their limitations, especially when you want to provide real-time information, respond to user actions, or create engaging user interfaces. Dynamic content enables you to:

1. **Real-Time Updates**: Display live data without the need to refresh the entire page, such as stock market prices, social media feeds, or chat applications.

2. **User Interaction**: Enhance user experience by responding to user actions like clicks, form submissions, or mouse movements.

3. **Customization**: Personalize content based on user preferences or choices, such as recommendations on e-commerce websites.

JavaScript for Dynamic Content

JavaScript is a versatile programming language that empowers you to create dynamic web content. Here are some common techniques for creating dynamic content with JavaScript:

InnerHTML and TextContent

As discussed in previous sections, you can use the innerHTML and textContent properties to update the content of HTML elements. This is useful for replacing text, inserting new elements, or altering the structure of a page dynamically.

```
var element = document.getElementById('myElement');

// Replace the content of the element
element.innerHTML = '<strong>New content</strong>';
```

Creating Elements

JavaScript allows you to create new HTML elements and append them to the DOM. This is handy for adding dynamic elements like lists, tables, or pop-up notifications.

```
var newListElement = document.createElement('ul');
var listItem = document.createElement('li');
listItem.textContent = 'New item';
```

```
// Append the new elements to an existing element
newListElement.appendChild(listItem);
```

Event Listeners

Event listeners are crucial for creating interactivity. You can attach event listeners to HTML elements to respond to user actions like clicks, mouseover events, or form submissions.

```
var button = document.getElementById('myButton');
var contentDiv = document.getElementById('contentDiv');

button.addEventListener('click', function() {
    // Change the content when the button is clicked
    contentDiv.innerHTML = 'Button clicked!';
});
```

AJAX and Fetch API

To fetch data from external sources or APIs without reloading the page, you can use technologies like AJAX (Asynchronous JavaScript and XML) or the modern Fetch API.

```
fetch('https://api.example.com/data')
    .then(response => response.json())
    .then(data => {
        // Use the fetched data to update the content
    })
    .catch(error => {
        console.error('Error fetching data:', error);
    });
```

Building Dynamic Web Pages

Creating dynamic content with JavaScript opens up countless possibilities in web development. You can build interactive forms, real-time dashboards, news tickers, or any web application that requires real-time updates and user engagement. Understanding these techniques is essential for modern web developers aiming to create dynamic and responsive web experiences.

Section 7.2: Form Handling and Validation

Forms are a fundamental part of web applications, enabling user input and interaction. JavaScript is commonly used to handle form submissions and validate user input. In this section, we'll explore how to work with forms effectively using JavaScript.

The Importance of Form Handling

Forms are used for various purposes, such as user registration, login, search, and data submission. Proper form handling ensures that user input is processed accurately and securely. JavaScript is instrumental in enhancing form functionality and user experience.

Accessing Form Elements

Before we can handle a form, we need to access its elements using JavaScript. You can use the getElementById, querySelector, or other DOM traversal techniques to retrieve form elements by their IDs, names, or other attributes.

```
var usernameInput = document.getElementById('username');
var emailInput = document.querySelector('input[name="email"]');
```

Form Submission

JavaScript allows you to intercept and customize form submissions. You can use event listeners to capture the form's submit event and execute custom code before the form is actually submitted to the server.

```
var form = document.getElementById('myForm');

form.addEventListener('submit', function(event) {
    // Prevent the default form submission
    event.preventDefault();

    // Custom validation and processing code
    var username = usernameInput.value;
    var email = emailInput.value;

    // Perform validation
    if (username === '' || email === '') {
        alert('Please fill in all fields.');
    } else {
        // Submit the form to the server or perform other actions
        form.submit();
    }
});
```

In the example above, the form's submit event is intercepted, preventing the default behavior (i.e., submitting the form to the server). Custom validation is performed, and the form can be submitted programmatically if the validation passes.

Form Validation

Form validation is essential to ensure that users provide correct and complete information. JavaScript is commonly used to validate user input on the client side before the form is submitted to the server.

Built-In Validation

HTML5 introduced built-in validation attributes like `required`, `type`, and `pattern` that help validate form fields without JavaScript. For example, you can use `required` to make a field mandatory.

```
<input type="text" name="username" id="username" required>
```

Custom Validation

For more complex validation logic, you can use JavaScript to check user input. Common validation tasks include checking for:

- Valid email addresses
- Minimum and maximum input lengths
- Numeric input for age, phone numbers, or quantities
- Password strength

```javascript
function validateEmail(email) {
    var regex = /^[a-zA-Z0-9._-]+@[a-zA-Z0-9.-]+\.[a-zA-Z-Z]{2,4}$/;
    return regex.test(email);
}

// Example usage
if (!validateEmail(emailInput.value)) {
    alert('Invalid email address');
}
```

Real-Time Validation

You can also provide real-time feedback to users as they fill out a form. Event listeners can be used to validate and provide instant feedback, such as indicating if a password is strong enough or if an email address is valid as the user types.

```javascript
passwordInput.addEventListener('input', function() {
    var password = passwordInput.value;

    // Check password strength and provide feedback
    if (isStrongPassword(password)) {
        passwordStrengthIndicator.textContent = 'Strong';
        passwordStrengthIndicator.style.color = 'green';
    } else {
        passwordStrengthIndicator.textContent = 'Weak';
        passwordStrengthIndicator.style.color = 'red';
    }
});
```

Conclusion

Form handling and validation are crucial aspects of web development, ensuring that user input is accurate and secure. JavaScript empowers developers to customize form behavior, perform client-side validation, and provide real-time feedback to users, ultimately enhancing the user experience and the reliability of web applications. Understanding these techniques is essential for building effective and user-friendly web forms.

Section 7.3: Working with Cookies and Local Storage

In web development, maintaining user data and preferences across sessions is essential for creating a personalized and user-friendly experience. Two common client-side storage mechanisms for achieving this are cookies and local storage. In this section, we'll explore how to work with cookies and local storage using JavaScript.

Cookies

Cookies are small pieces of data that a web server sends to a user's browser, and the browser stores them locally. Cookies can persist across browser sessions and are often used for tasks like user authentication, tracking user behavior, and storing user preferences.

Creating Cookies

JavaScript allows you to create cookies by setting values in the document.cookie property. A cookie typically consists of a name-value pair, but you can also include additional attributes like expiration date, path, and domain.

```
// Create a simple cookie
document.cookie = 'username=John';

// Create a cookie with attributes
document.cookie = 'username=John; expires=Fri, 31 Dec 2023 23:59:59 GMT;
path=/';
```

Reading Cookies

To read cookies, you can access the document.cookie property. However, this property contains all cookies for the current website as a single string, so you need to parse it to retrieve specific cookie values.

```
// Read all cookies
var allCookies = document.cookie;

// Parse and access a specific cookie
function getCookie(name) {
    var cookies = document.cookie.split('; ');
    for (var i = 0; i < cookies.length; i++) {
        var cookie = cookies[i].split('=');
        if (cookie[0] === name) {
            return cookie[1];
        }
    }
```

```
        }
        return null;
}

var username = getCookie('username');
```

Modifying and Deleting Cookies

You can modify existing cookies by reassigning them with new values or attributes. To delete a cookie, set its expiration date to a past date.

```
// Modify a cookie
document.cookie = 'username=NewValue; expires=Fri, 31 Dec 2023 23:59:59 GMT; path=/';

// Delete a cookie (by setting expiration to the past)
document.cookie = 'username=; expires=Thu, 01 Jan 1970 00:00:00 GMT; path=/';
```

Local Storage

Local storage is a client-side storage mechanism that allows you to store key-value pairs in the user's browser. Unlike cookies, local storage has a larger capacity (typically around 5-10MB per domain) and is not sent to the server with every HTTP request, making it suitable for storing user preferences and application data.

Storing and Retrieving Data

You can use the localStorage object to store and retrieve data in local storage. Data is stored as strings, so you'll need to convert objects to JSON and back when working with complex data types.

```
// Storing data in local storage
localStorage.setItem('username', 'John');
localStorage.setItem('userAge', '30');

// Retrieving data from local storage
var username = localStorage.getItem('username');
var userAge = localStorage.getItem('userAge');
```

Removing Data

To remove data from local storage, you can use the removeItem method to delete a specific key-value pair or the clear method to clear all data for the current domain.

```
// Remove a specific item
localStorage.removeItem('username');

// Clear all data for the current domain
localStorage.clear();
```

Choosing Between Cookies and Local Storage

When deciding between cookies and local storage, consider the following:

- **Purpose**: Cookies are often used for authentication and server-side tracking, while local storage is more suitable for client-side data storage and preferences.
- **Storage Limit**: Cookies have a smaller storage limit (typically around 4KB per cookie) compared to local storage.
- **Security**: Local storage is more secure because data is not sent to the server with every request, reducing the risk of data interception.
- **Expiration**: Cookies can have an expiration date, while data in local storage can persist indefinitely.

Understanding when and how to use cookies and local storage is crucial for building web applications that offer a seamless and personalized user experience. Each storage mechanism has its advantages and limitations, and the choice depends on your specific use case and requirements.

Section 7.4: AJAX and Fetch API for Data Exchange

Asynchronous JavaScript and XML (AJAX) and the Fetch API are essential tools for making network requests and exchanging data between a web page and a server without the need for a full page refresh. This capability is crucial for creating interactive and dynamic web applications. In this section, we'll explore AJAX and the modern Fetch API.

AJAX (Asynchronous JavaScript and XML)

AJAX is a set of web development techniques that allows you to update parts of a web page without the need to reload the entire page. It enables asynchronous communication with a server, making it possible to retrieve data, send data, and update the user interface in real time.

XMLHttpRequest

Traditionally, AJAX was implemented using the XMLHttpRequest object, which provides methods for making HTTP requests and handling responses.

```
var xhr = new XMLHttpRequest();
xhr.open('GET', 'https://api.example.com/data', true);

xhr.onreadystatechange = function() {
    if (xhr.readyState === 4 && xhr.status === 200) {
        var data = JSON.parse(xhr.responseText);
        // Process and use the retrieved data
    }
};
```

```
xhr.send();
```

In this example, we create an XMLHttpRequest object, configure it for a GET request, specify the URL, and set up an event listener to handle the response when it's received. Once the data is retrieved, it can be processed and used to update the web page.

Fetch API

The Fetch API is a more modern and user-friendly way to make network requests. It provides a more straightforward and promise-based approach to working with network data.

```
fetch('https://api.example.com/data')
    .then(function(response) {
        if (!response.ok) {
            throw new Error('Network response was not ok');
        }
        return response.json();
    })
    .then(function(data) {
        // Process and use the retrieved data
    })
    .catch(function(error) {
        // Handle errors
    });
```

With the Fetch API, you use the fetch function to initiate a request and then chain then and catch methods to handle the response or any errors. This approach simplifies asynchronous data retrieval and error handling.

Cross-Origin Requests

When making requests to a different domain (cross-origin requests), you may encounter cross-origin restrictions enforced by web browsers. To enable cross-origin requests, you can use techniques like Cross-Origin Resource Sharing (CORS) on the server or JSONP (JSON with Padding) for certain scenarios.

Asynchronous Operations

Both AJAX and the Fetch API are asynchronous, meaning that they don't block the main thread of the web page. This allows for smooth user interactions even while data is being fetched or sent to the server.

Conclusion

AJAX and the Fetch API are essential tools for creating dynamic and responsive web applications. They enable data exchange between the client and server, opening the door to real-time updates, interactive forms, and more. While AJAX with XMLHttpRequest is still widely used, the Fetch API offers a more modern and user-friendly approach for making network requests and handling responses. Understanding how to use these techniques is crucial for building modern web applications.

Section 7.5: Creating Interactive Web Forms

Web forms play a vital role in gathering user input on websites, from user registrations to search queries and feedback submissions. In this section, we will explore the creation of interactive web forms, including form validation, user feedback, and best practices for enhancing the user experience.

Building a Web Form

Creating a basic web form involves using HTML's `<form>` element to define the form structure. Inside the form, you can include various input fields like text fields, radio buttons, checkboxes, dropdowns, and buttons.

```
<form action="submit.php" method="post">
    <label for="name">Name:</label>
    <input type="text" id="name" name="name" required>

    <label for="email">Email:</label>
    <input type="email" id="email" name="email" required>

    <label for="message">Message:</label>
    <textarea id="message" name="message" rows="4" required></textarea>

    <input type="submit" value="Submit">
</form>
```

In this example, we have a simple form that collects the user's name, email address, and a message. The `required` attribute is used to ensure that these fields are filled out before submission.

Form Validation

Validating user input is crucial to ensure that the data submitted through a form is accurate and conforms to the expected format. JavaScript can be used to perform client-side validation, providing instant feedback to users.

```
document.getElementById('myForm').addEventListener('submit', function(event)
{
    var name = document.getElementById('name').value;
    var email = document.getElementById('email').value;

    if (name === '' || email === '' || !isValidEmail(email)) {
        alert('Please fill out all fields and provide a valid email
address.');
        event.preventDefault(); // Prevent form submission
```

```
    }
});

function isValidEmail(email) {
    // Implement email validation logic
    // Regular expressions or other methods can be used here
    return true; // Return true if email is valid, false otherwise
}
```

In this code, we add an event listener to the form's submit event. When the form is submitted, the JavaScript code checks if the name and email fields are empty and if the email is valid. If any validation condition fails, an alert is displayed, and `event.preventDefault()` prevents the form from being submitted.

Enhancing User Experience

Enhancing the user experience involves providing clear instructions, using proper form labels and placeholders, and offering real-time feedback as users interact with the form. Additionally, you can improve accessibility by ensuring that form elements are keyboard-navigable and properly labeled.

Server-Side Validation

While client-side validation is valuable for improving the user experience, it's essential to perform server-side validation as well. Server-side validation ensures that submitted data is valid and secure on the server, preventing potential security vulnerabilities and data integrity issues.

Handling Form Submissions

Once a form is submitted and validated, the data can be sent to a server for processing. Server-side scripts, such as PHP or Node.js, can handle form submissions, process the data, and store it in a database or take other relevant actions.

```php
<?php
if ($_SERVER['REQUEST_METHOD'] === 'POST') {
    $name = $_POST['name'];
    $email = $_POST['email'];
    $message = $_POST['message'];

    // Process and store the data as needed
}
?>
```

In this PHP example, the server receives the form data via the $_POST superglobal array and can perform actions such as sending email notifications or saving the data to a database.

Creating interactive web forms that provide a smooth user experience and robust data validation is a fundamental skill for web developers. Proper form design and validation contribute to user satisfaction and the overall functionality of web applications.

Chapter 8: JQuery Framework

Section 8.1: Introduction to JQuery

jQuery is a popular JavaScript library that simplifies HTML document traversal, manipulation, event handling, and animation. It was created to make web development tasks easier and more efficient by providing a simple and consistent API for working with the Document Object Model (DOM) and handling common web development tasks. In this section, we'll introduce you to the basics of jQuery and how to get started using it in your web projects.

Why Use jQuery?

jQuery became popular because it significantly simplifies working with JavaScript and the DOM. Here are some key reasons why developers choose to use jQuery:

1. **Simplified DOM Manipulation:** jQuery provides a concise and easy-to-use syntax for selecting and manipulating DOM elements. You can perform tasks like adding, removing, or modifying elements with minimal code.

2. **Cross-Browser Compatibility:** jQuery abstracts the differences in how browsers implement JavaScript, ensuring that your code works consistently across various browsers.

3. **Event Handling:** jQuery simplifies event handling by providing a unified way to attach event listeners to elements. This makes it easier to respond to user interactions.

4. **AJAX Support:** jQuery includes built-in functions for making asynchronous requests, simplifying data retrieval from servers.

5. **Animation and Effects:** You can create smooth animations and add visual effects to your web pages using jQuery's animation functions.

Getting Started with jQuery

To use jQuery in your web project, you need to include the jQuery library in your HTML document. You can either download the library and host it on your server or include it from a content delivery network (CDN). Here's an example of how to include jQuery from a CDN:

```
<!DOCTYPE html>
<html>
<head>
    <title>My Web Page</title>
    <script src="https://code.jquery.com/jquery-3.6.0.min.js"></script>
</head>
<body>
    <!-- Your HTML content here -->
```

```
</body>
</html>
```

Once jQuery is included, you can start using its features by writing JavaScript code. Here's a simple example that selects an HTML element and changes its text content:

```
$(document).ready(function() {
    // Wait for the document to be ready
    // Select an element with the ID "myElement" and change its text
    $("#myElement").text("Hello, jQuery!");
});
```

In this example, we use the `$(document).ready()` function to ensure that our code runs after the DOM is fully loaded. We then use the `$()` function (often referred to as the jQuery selector) to select an element with the ID "myElement" and change its text content.

Conclusion

jQuery is a powerful and versatile JavaScript library that simplifies many common web development tasks. It provides a consistent and efficient way to work with the DOM, handle events, and create dynamic and interactive web pages. In the following sections, we will delve deeper into various aspects of jQuery and explore how it can be used to enhance your web projects.

Section 8.2: Selecting and Manipulating Elements with JQuery

jQuery's core functionality revolves around selecting and manipulating elements within an HTML document. In this section, we'll explore how jQuery allows you to select elements and perform various operations on them.

Selecting Elements

jQuery provides a powerful and flexible way to select HTML elements, similar to CSS selectors. You can select elements by their tag name, class, ID, attributes, and more. Here are some common ways to select elements using jQuery:

- **By Tag Name:** To select all `<p>` elements on a page, you can use `$("p")`.

- **By Class:** To select all elements with a specific class, you can use `$(".classname")`.

- **By ID:** To select an element by its ID, you can use `$("#elementID")`.

- **By Attribute:** You can select elements based on attributes, such as `$("input[type='text']")` to select all text input fields.

- **Combining Selectors:** You can combine selectors to target specific elements more precisely. For example, `$("ul li")` selects all `<li>` elements within `<ul>` elements.

Manipulating Elements

Once you've selected one or more elements, jQuery allows you to manipulate them easily. Here are some common operations you can perform:

1. Changing Content

You can change the content of elements, such as text, HTML, or attributes. For example:

```
$("#myElement").text("New text"); // Change text content
$("#myElement").html("<strong>Updated</strong> content"); // Change HTML
content
$("#myImage").attr("src", "new-image.jpg"); // Change an attribute (src in
this case)
```

2. Adding and Removing Elements

You can add new elements to the DOM or remove existing ones:

```
// Adding a new element
$("<p>New paragraph</p>").appendTo("#myContainer");

// Removing an element
$("#toBeRemoved").remove();
```

3. Modifying CSS

You can change CSS properties and apply styles to elements:

```
$("#myElement").css("color", "red"); // Change text color
$("#myElement").addClass("highlight"); // Add a CSS class
$("#myElement").removeClass("highlight"); // Remove a CSS class
```

4. Events and Event Handling

jQuery simplifies event handling. You can attach event listeners to elements:

```
$("#myButton").click(function() {
    alert("Button clicked!");
});
```

5. Animations and Effects

jQuery provides animation functions for creating smooth transitions and effects:

```
$("#myElement").slideUp(); // Slide up animation
$("#myElement").fadeIn(); // Fade in animation
```

Conclusion

jQuery's ability to select and manipulate elements simplifies web development significantly. It provides a concise and consistent API for working with the DOM, making it easier to create interactive and dynamic web pages. In the next sections, we'll explore more advanced topics in jQuery, including event handling, AJAX requests, and extending jQuery with plugins.

Section 8.3: Event Handling and Animation with JQuery

Event handling and animation are essential aspects of web development that can greatly enhance the user experience. In this section, we'll delve into how jQuery simplifies event handling and provides tools for creating animations and effects on your web pages.

Event Handling

jQuery makes it easy to handle user interactions and events, such as clicks, mouse movements, keyboard input, and more. Here's a brief overview of how event handling works in jQuery:

1. Event Binding

You can bind event handlers to elements using jQuery's event methods. For example, to handle a click event on a button with the ID "myButton," you can use the following code:

```
$("#myButton").click(function() {
    alert("Button clicked!");
});
```

2. Event Delegation

Event delegation is a technique that allows you to attach a single event handler to a parent element and have it respond to events on its child elements. This is especially useful for dynamically created elements. Here's an example:

```
$("#parentElement").on("click", "button", function() {
    alert("Button clicked!");
});
```

3. Common Events

jQuery provides shortcuts for common events like click, hover, focus, and more. Here are some examples:

```
$("#myElement").click(function() {
    // Handle click event
});

$("#myElement").hover(
    function() {
        // Handle mouse enter
    },
    function() {
        // Handle mouse leave
```

```
    }
);

$("#myInput").focus(function() {
    // Handle focus event
});
```

4. Event Object

Event handlers receive an event object that provides information about the event, such as the target element and event type. You can use this object to perform specific actions based on the event.

Animation and Effects

jQuery simplifies the creation of animations and effects, allowing you to add dynamic and interactive elements to your web pages. Here are some animation and effect functions provided by jQuery:

1. Basic Animation
```
$("#myElement").slideUp(); // Slide up animation
$("#myElement").fadeIn(); // Fade in animation
```

2. Custom Animations

You can create custom animations by changing CSS properties over time. For example:

```
$("#myElement").animate({
    left: '250px',
    opacity: '0.5'
}, 1000); // Move left and change opacity over 1 second
```

3. Chaining Animations

jQuery allows you to chain animations, creating sequences of effects. Here's an example:

```
$("#myElement")
    .slideUp()
    .slideDown()
    .fadeOut()
    .fadeIn();
```

4. Callbacks

You can specify callback functions to execute after animations or effects complete:

```
$("#myElement").fadeOut(1000, function() {
    alert("Animation complete!");
});
```

Conclusion

jQuery simplifies event handling and provides a wide range of animation and effect functions, making it a valuable tool for creating dynamic and interactive web pages. In the next sections, we will explore AJAX requests and how to extend jQuery's functionality using plugins.

Section 8.4: AJAX and Data Retrieval with JQuery

AJAX (Asynchronous JavaScript and XML) is a fundamental technology for making asynchronous requests to a server and retrieving data without requiring a full page reload. jQuery provides powerful AJAX methods that simplify data retrieval and interaction with web servers. In this section, we'll explore how to use jQuery for AJAX requests and data manipulation.

AJAX Basics

AJAX allows you to perform actions like sending HTTP requests (GET, POST, PUT, DELETE) and receiving responses from the server without refreshing the entire web page. jQuery's AJAX methods provide a convenient way to work with these requests.

Making GET Requests

To make a GET request using jQuery, you can use the `$.get()` method. Here's a simple example:

```
$.get("https://api.example.com/data", function(data) {
    console.log(data);
});
```

Making POST Requests

To make a POST request with data using jQuery, you can use the `$.post()` method:

```
$.post("https://api.example.com/submit", { name: "John", age: 30 },
function(response) {
    console.log(response);
});
```

Handling Responses

You can handle server responses in the callback function. The data parameter contains the server's response in the form of text, JSON, or XML, depending on the server's response type.

Working with JSON

Working with JSON is common in web development, especially when dealing with API data. jQuery simplifies JSON-related tasks.

Parsing JSON

To parse JSON data received from the server, you can use the `JSON.parse()` function or the `$.getJSON()` method:

```
$.getJSON("https://api.example.com/data", function(data) {
    console.log(data);
});
```

Sending JSON

When sending data to the server in JSON format, you need to stringify your JavaScript object:

```
var postData = { name: "John", age: 30 };
$.ajax({
    url: "https://api.example.com/submit",
    type: "POST",
    data: JSON.stringify(postData),
    contentType: "application/json",
    success: function(response) {
        console.log(response);
    }
});
```

Handling Errors

Error handling is crucial in AJAX requests. You can handle errors using the `error` callback:

```
$.get("https://api.example.com/data", function(data) {
    console.log(data);
}).fail(function(error) {
    console.error("Request failed:", error);
});
```

Conclusion

jQuery simplifies AJAX requests and data manipulation, making it easier to interact with web servers and retrieve data asynchronously. This capability is essential for building dynamic and responsive web applications. In the next section, we'll explore how to extend jQuery's functionality using plugins.

Section 8.5: Extending JQuery with Plugins

jQuery's extensibility is one of its key strengths. Developers can create and use plugins to add new functionality or enhance existing features. In this section, we'll explore how to extend jQuery with plugins and leverage the vast library of plugins available in the jQuery ecosystem.

What Are jQuery Plugins?

jQuery plugins are pieces of code that extend the functionality of jQuery. They encapsulate specific features or behaviors, making it easy to reuse them across different projects. Plugins can range from simple UI enhancements to complex data manipulation tools.

Using jQuery Plugins

To use a jQuery plugin, you typically follow these steps:

1. **Include jQuery**: Ensure that you've included the jQuery library on your web page. Most plugins require jQuery to function.

2. **Include the Plugin**: Include the plugin script after jQuery in your HTML file. You can do this by adding a script tag that references the plugin file.

3. **Invoke the Plugin**: Initialize the plugin on the HTML elements you want to enhance. This is usually done using a jQuery selector and the plugin's function or method.

Here's a simple example of using a hypothetical "datepicker" jQuery plugin:

```html
<!DOCTYPE html>
<html>
<head>
    <title>Using jQuery Plugin</title>
    <script src="jquery.min.js"></script> <!-- Include jQuery -->
    <script src="datepicker-plugin.js"></script> <!-- Include the plugin -->
</head>
<body>
    <input type="text" id="date-input">
    <script>
        $(document).ready(function() {
            // Initialize the datepicker plugin
            $("#date-input").datepicker();
        });
    </script>
</body>
</html>
```

Popular jQuery Plugins

jQuery's plugin ecosystem offers a wide range of solutions for various web development needs. Here are some popular types of jQuery plugins:

1. UI Widgets

Plugins like datepickers, sliders, and tooltips enhance the user interface of web applications.

2. Form Validation

Form validation plugins help validate user inputs and provide feedback for better user experiences.

3. Lightboxes and Modals

These plugins create pop-up windows and lightboxes for displaying images, videos, or other content.

4. Carousel and Slideshow

Carousel and slideshow plugins allow you to create image galleries and presentations.

5. Charts and Graphs

Plugins like Chart.js and Flot enable you to create interactive charts and graphs.

6. AJAX Loaders

These plugins simplify AJAX loading and provide loading animations or spinners.

7. Lazy Loading

Lazy loading plugins improve page load times by loading images or content as users scroll down the page.

8. Social Media Integration

Plugins for integrating social media feeds and sharing buttons into websites.

9. Data Tables

Data table plugins make it easy to create and manage tables with advanced features like sorting and filtering.

Conclusion

jQuery's extensibility through plugins makes it a versatile tool for web developers. By leveraging existing plugins or creating custom ones, you can add advanced functionality to your web applications efficiently. Always ensure that plugins are well-documented and regularly updated to maintain compatibility with newer versions of jQuery. In the next chapters, we'll explore best practices for web design and development.

Chapter 9: Web Design Best Practices

Section 9.1: User-Centered Design Principles

User-centered design (UCD) is a fundamental concept in web design and development that prioritizes the needs and preferences of users. The primary goal of UCD is to create websites and web applications that are user-friendly, efficient, and enjoyable to use. In this section, we'll delve into the principles and strategies of user-centered design and how they can be applied to enhance the user experience.

Understanding User-Centered Design (UCD)

User-centered design is an iterative process that involves continuous collaboration with end-users throughout the design and development lifecycle. Its core principles include:

1. **User Empathy**: Understanding the needs, goals, and pain points of your target audience is crucial. Conduct user research, surveys, and interviews to gain insights.

2. **Usability**: Ensure that your website or application is easy to navigate and use. Intuitive interfaces and clear, concise content are key.

3. **Iteration**: UCD involves constant refinement based on user feedback. It's not a one-time process but an ongoing commitment to improvement.

4. **Accessibility**: Make your digital products accessible to users with disabilities by adhering to accessibility standards such as WCAG (Web Content Accessibility Guidelines).

5. **Consistency**: Maintain consistency in design elements, layout, and interaction patterns to create a cohesive user experience.

User-Centered Design Process

The UCD process typically consists of the following stages:

1. **Research**: *Gather information about your target audience, their needs, and the context in which they'll use your website or application.*

2. **Planning**: *Define the project scope, objectives, and goals. Create user personas to represent different user groups.*

3. **Design**: *Create wireframes, prototypes, and design mockups. Test these designs with users to gather feedback.*

4. **Development**: *Build the website or application based on the approved design. Implement features that align with user needs and preferences.*

5. **Testing**: *Conduct usability testing to identify issues and areas for improvement. Make necessary revisions.*

6. **Launch**: *Deploy the final product and monitor its performance. Gather post-launch feedback from users.*

7. **Iteration**: *Continuously refine and enhance the product based on user feedback and changing requirements.*

Usability Testing

Usability testing is a critical aspect of UCD. It involves observing real users as they interact with your website or application. Key aspects of usability testing include:

- **Task Scenarios**: Create scenarios that reflect common user tasks and observe how users navigate and complete them.

- **Think Aloud**: Encourage users to verbalize their thoughts, feelings, and reactions as they interact with your design.

- **Data Collection**: Collect both qualitative and quantitative data on user interactions and satisfaction.

- **Iterative Improvement**: Use the findings from usability testing to make iterative improvements to your design.

Conclusion

User-centered design principles are fundamental to creating web experiences that meet the needs and expectations of your audience. By adopting a user-centric approach and continuously seeking user feedback, you can design and develop websites and applications that are more engaging, effective, and user-friendly. In the following sections, we'll explore additional best practices in web design and development, including accessibility and cross-browser compatibility.

Section 9.2: Accessibility and Inclusive Design

Accessibility is a fundamental aspect of web design and development that ensures all users, including those with disabilities, can access and use digital content. Inclusive design goes hand in hand with accessibility, aiming to create web experiences that are welcoming and usable by the widest possible audience. In this section, we'll explore the importance of accessibility and the principles of inclusive design.

The Importance of Accessibility

Web accessibility is not only a legal requirement in many countries but also a moral and ethical responsibility. It's about ensuring that everyone, regardless of their abilities, can use and benefit from your website or application. Accessibility considerations are particularly important for individuals with:

- **Visual Disabilities**: Blindness, low vision, color blindness, etc.
- **Hearing Disabilities**: Deafness or hard of hearing.
- **Motor Disabilities**: Difficulty using a mouse or keyboard.
- **Cognitive Disabilities**: Learning disabilities, ADHD, etc.

Principles of Inclusive Design

Inclusive design goes beyond compliance with accessibility standards; it focuses on creating a truly inclusive and welcoming digital environment. Here are some key principles:

1. **Universal Design**: Strive to design for all users from the beginning. Avoid creating separate accessible versions of your website.

2. **Perceivable Information**: Ensure that all content can be perceived in multiple ways. Provide alternative text for images, captions for videos, and text-based alternatives for non-text content.

3. **Operable Interfaces**: Make sure your website is navigable and usable using a keyboard or other assistive devices. Ensure that interactive elements are clearly labeled and easy to operate.

4. **Understandable Content**: Present content in a clear and organized manner. Use plain language and avoid jargon. Provide instructions and error messages that are easy to understand.

5. **Robust and Reliable**: Ensure your website works with a variety of assistive technologies and is compatible with different web browsers and devices. Regularly test for compatibility.

The Web Content Accessibility Guidelines (WCAG) provide a set of internationally recognized standards for web accessibility. They are organized into three levels of conformance: A, AA, and AAA. Level AA is commonly used as a minimum requirement for web accessibility compliance. Some key WCAG guidelines include:

- Providing alternative text for images and non-text content.
- Ensuring keyboard accessibility for all interactive elements.
- Making text content adaptable and readable.
- Providing clear and consistent navigation and page structure.

Practical Implementation

Implementing accessibility and inclusive design involves various technical and design considerations. Some common practices include:

- Using semantic HTML elements to provide structure and meaning to content.
- Adding ARIA (Accessible Rich Internet Applications) attributes to enhance the accessibility of dynamic content.
- Testing your website with assistive technologies like screen readers to identify and fix issues.

Conclusion

Accessibility and inclusive design are integral to creating a web that is truly for everyone. By prioritizing accessibility from the beginning of your web development process and following best practices, you can ensure that your digital content is inclusive, welcoming, and usable by a diverse audience. In the next sections, we'll explore additional aspects of web design, including cross-browser compatibility and performance optimization.

Section 9.3: Cross-Browser Compatibility

Cross-browser compatibility is a critical consideration in web design and development. It ensures that your website or web application functions correctly and consistently across different web browsers and versions. In this section, we'll explore the importance of cross-browser compatibility and strategies to achieve it.

Why Cross-Browser Compatibility Matters

The web is accessed by users using a variety of web browsers, including Google Chrome, Mozilla Firefox, Apple Safari, Microsoft Edge, and others. Each browser interprets and renders web content differently, which can lead to inconsistencies and issues if your website is not designed to accommodate these variations. Here's why cross-browser compatibility is essential:

1. **User Experience**: Inconsistent rendering can frustrate users and lead to a poor experience on your website.

2. **Audience Reach**: Limiting your website to a specific browser can exclude potential visitors who prefer other browsers.

3. **Professionalism**: A website that works well across all browsers demonstrates professionalism and attention to detail.

Strategies for Cross-Browser Compatibility

Achieving cross-browser compatibility requires a combination of best practices and testing. Here are some strategies to ensure your web project works smoothly across browsers:

1. **Use Modern Web Standards**: Develop your website following web standards such as HTML5, CSS3, and JavaScript ECMAScript 6 (ES6). Modern browsers have better support for these standards.

2. **Progressive Enhancement**: Start with a basic, functional version of your website that works in older browsers. Then, add enhancements and features that take advantage of modern browser capabilities.

3. **Feature Detection**: Use feature detection techniques to identify browser capabilities before applying certain styles or functionality. Libraries like Modernizr can help with this.

4. **Responsive Design**: Implement responsive web design principles to ensure your site adapts to different screen sizes and resolutions.

5. **Testing**: Regularly test your website in multiple browsers and their different versions. Consider using browser testing tools or services to automate this process.

6. **Polyfills**: For older browsers that lack support for certain features (e.g., CSS Grid or ES6 features), consider using polyfills or libraries that provide equivalent functionality.

Common Cross-Browser Issues

Some common cross-browser issues include:

- **CSS Compatibility**: Differences in CSS rendering can lead to layout and styling issues. Use browser-specific CSS hacks sparingly and prefer standard CSS solutions.

- **JavaScript Compatibility**: Be aware of JavaScript differences, especially when using ES6 features. Test thoroughly and use transpilers like Babel if needed.

- **HTML and DOM Differences**: Differences in how browsers parse and render HTML can cause unexpected behavior. Validate your HTML and use JavaScript libraries like jQuery to abstract DOM manipulations when necessary.

- **Performance Variations**: Some browsers may perform better or worse with certain web technologies. Optimize your website for performance across the most popular browsers.

Conclusion

Cross-browser compatibility is essential for ensuring a consistent and positive user experience on your website. By adhering to web standards, employing progressive enhancement, and thoroughly testing your site across different browsers, you can minimize compatibility issues and reach a broader audience. In the next sections, we'll explore additional aspects of web design, including performance optimization and debugging and testing techniques.

Section 9.4: Performance Optimization Techniques

Performance optimization is a crucial aspect of web design and development. A fast and responsive website not only improves the user experience but also contributes to higher search engine rankings and user engagement. In this section, we'll explore various techniques to optimize the performance of your website.

Why Performance Optimization Matters

Website performance directly impacts user satisfaction and business success. Here are some reasons why performance optimization is essential:

1. **User Experience**: Slow-loading websites frustrate users and lead to higher bounce rates.

2. **SEO Benefits**: Search engines consider page speed as a ranking factor. Faster websites are more likely to appear higher in search results.

3. **Conversion Rates**: Improved performance can lead to higher conversion rates, resulting in more sales or leads.

4. **Cost Savings**: Faster websites require fewer server resources, leading to reduced hosting costs.

Performance Optimization Techniques

Achieving optimal website performance involves a combination of strategies and best practices. Here are some techniques to consider:

1. **Image Optimization**: Compress and optimize images to reduce file sizes without compromising quality. Use modern image formats like WebP when possible.

2. **Lazy Loading**: Implement lazy loading for images and other non-critical resources. This loads content as users scroll, reducing initial load times.

3. **Content Delivery Network (CDN)**: Use a CDN to distribute website assets to servers around the world, reducing latency and speeding up content delivery.

4. **Minification**: Minify HTML, CSS, and JavaScript files by removing unnecessary whitespace, comments, and formatting. Smaller files load faster.

5. **Browser Caching**: Leverage browser caching to store static assets locally on users' devices. This reduces the need to re-download files on subsequent visits.

6. **Content Compression**: Enable server-side compression (e.g., GZIP) to reduce the size of transferred data.

7. **Reduce HTTP Requests**: Minimize the number of HTTP requests by combining CSS and JavaScript files, using image sprites, and loading scripts asynchronously.

8. **Responsive Design**: Implement responsive design to serve optimized content for different screen sizes, reducing the amount of unnecessary data transferred to mobile devices.

9. **Use a Content Management System (CMS) Wisely**: CMS platforms can introduce bloat. Only install necessary plugins and keep the system and plugins up to date.

10. **Code Splitting**: Divide JavaScript into smaller, more manageable chunks and load them only when needed, improving initial page load times.

Testing and Monitoring

After implementing these optimization techniques, it's essential to continuously test and monitor your website's performance. Use tools like Google PageSpeed Insights, GTmetrix, or WebPageTest to analyze your site's speed and identify areas for improvement.

Conclusion

Performance optimization is an ongoing process that significantly impacts user satisfaction, search engine ranking, and overall website success. By implementing the techniques mentioned above and regularly testing and monitoring your website's performance, you can ensure that it loads quickly and provides a smooth experience for users. In the next sections, we'll explore debugging and testing techniques for web pages.

Section 9.5: Debugging and Testing Web Pages

Debugging and testing are integral parts of the web development process. They ensure that your web pages function correctly, display properly across different devices and browsers, and deliver a seamless user experience. In this section, we'll explore various debugging and testing techniques to help you build robust and error-free web pages.

Debugging Techniques

1. **Browser Developer Tools**: Modern web browsers come with built-in developer tools that allow you to inspect HTML, CSS, and JavaScript, as well as debug code. You can set breakpoints, examine variables, and trace the flow of your scripts.

```javascript
// Example of setting a breakpoint in JavaScript
function calculateTotal(price, quantity) {
    debugger; // This triggers the debugger in the developer tools
    return price * quantity;
}
```

2. **Console Logging**: Use the console.log() function to output messages and variable values to the browser's console. This helps identify issues and understand the flow of your code.

```javascript
console.log('Page loaded successfully');
```

3. **Error Handling**: Implement proper error handling with try-catch blocks to gracefully handle exceptions and prevent your code from breaking.

```javascript
try {
    // Code that might throw an error
} catch (error) {
    console.error('An error occurred:', error);
}
```

Testing Techniques

1. **Cross-Browser Testing**: Test your web pages in different browsers and their versions to ensure compatibility. Tools like BrowserStack or cross-browser testing services can help.

2. **Responsive Design Testing**: Use emulators, browser extensions, or online tools to test how your web pages respond to different screen sizes and orientations.

3. **Mobile Testing**: Test on actual mobile devices or emulators to ensure a smooth experience for mobile users.

4. **Accessibility Testing**: Verify that your web pages are accessible to users with disabilities. Tools like WAVE or axe can help identify accessibility issues.

5. **Performance Testing**: Evaluate your website's speed and performance using tools like Google PageSpeed Insights or GTmetrix. Address any bottlenecks that may slow down your site.

Automated Testing

1. **Unit Testing**: Implement unit tests for individual components or functions of your web application. Tools like Jest or Mocha can help automate unit testing.

2. **Integration Testing**: Test the interactions between different components or modules of your web application. Tools like Cypress or Selenium are commonly used for integration testing.

3. **Continuous Integration (CI)**: Set up CI/CD pipelines to automate testing and deployment processes. Services like Travis CI or Jenkins can help automate testing whenever code changes are pushed.

User Testing

1. **Usability Testing**: Conduct usability tests with real users to gather feedback on the user interface and overall user experience. Tools like UsabilityHub or UserTesting.com can assist in user testing.

2. **Beta Testing**: Release a beta version of your website to a limited audience to gather feedback and identify potential issues before a full launch.

Conclusion

Debugging and testing are critical steps in the web development lifecycle. They ensure that your web pages are free of errors, accessible to all users, and perform well across various devices and browsers. By employing a combination of manual testing, automated testing, and user testing, you can create web pages that provide a seamless and enjoyable experience for your audience. In the following chapters, we'll delve into topics like responsive web design, CSS frameworks, and web typography.

Chapter 10: Responsive Web Design

Section 10.1: The Importance of Responsive Design

In today's digital landscape, the diversity of devices and screen sizes used to access the web has grown exponentially. Users browse websites on smartphones, tablets, laptops, desktops, smart TVs, and even wearables. To provide an optimal user experience across this wide array of devices, responsive web design has become essential.

Responsive web design is an approach that aims to make web pages render well on various devices and screen sizes by adapting the layout, content, and functionality. Here, we'll delve into why responsive design is crucial and explore its key concepts.

The Multi-Device Challenge

Before the era of responsive design, web developers faced a significant challenge: creating separate websites or versions for different devices. This approach was time-consuming, costly, and often led to inconsistencies in content and user experience. Responsive design addresses this challenge by offering a flexible and adaptable solution.

Key Concepts of Responsive Design

1. *Fluid Layouts*: Responsive design uses fluid grids that adapt to the width of the device's screen. This ensures that content flows naturally and doesn't get cut off, regardless of the viewport size.

```css
/* Example of a fluid grid with CSS */
.container {
    width: 100%;
    max-width: 1200px;
    margin: 0 auto;
}

.column {
    width: 100%;
    padding: 1em;
    box-sizing: border-box;
}
```

2. *Media Queries*: Media queries are CSS rules that allow you to apply different styles based on the characteristics of the device, such as screen width, height, or orientation.

```css
/* Example of a media query for screens smaller than 768px */
@media (max-width: 768px) {
    .column {
        width: 50%;
    }
}
```

3. **Flexible Images and Media**: *Images and media elements should scale proportionally to fit the screen. You can achieve this using CSS properties like max-width: 100%; to ensure images don't overflow their containers.*

```
/* Ensuring images scale proportionally */
img {
    max-width: 100%;
    height: auto;
}
```

4. **Mobile-First Approach**: *This design philosophy involves starting the design process with mobile devices in mind and progressively enhancing the layout and features for larger screens. It ensures a strong mobile experience and simplifies scaling up.*

Benefits of Responsive Design

1. **Improved User Experience**: *Users can access your website on their preferred device without sacrificing usability. Content adapts to different screens, making it easy to read and navigate.*

2. **SEO-Friendly**: *Search engines like Google prioritize mobile-friendly websites in their rankings. Responsive design can positively impact your site's SEO performance.*

3. **Cost-Efficient**: *Maintaining a single responsive website is more cost-effective than managing multiple versions for different devices.*

4. **Future-Proofing**: *As new devices with varying screen sizes emerge, a responsive design approach ensures your website remains accessible and functional.*

In the subsequent sections of this chapter, we'll explore the technical aspects of implementing responsive design, including media queries, flexible grids, and testing methods to ensure your website looks great on all devices.

Section 10.2: Media Queries for Different Devices

Media queries are a fundamental aspect of responsive web design. They enable you to apply specific CSS rules based on the characteristics of the device or viewport. In Section 10.1, we introduced the concept of media queries. Now, we'll dive deeper into how to use them effectively to target different devices.

Basic Syntax of Media Queries

Media queries use the @media rule in CSS to define conditions for applying styles. The basic syntax looks like this:

```
@media (condition) {
    /* CSS rules to apply when the condition is met */
}
```

Here, `condition` specifies the criteria for when the styles inside the media query should be applied. For responsive design, you'll most commonly use conditions based on the viewport width, height, or orientation.

Targeting Different Screen Widths

One of the most common uses of media queries is to create responsive layouts that adapt to various screen widths. For example, you can define different styles for small screens (e.g., smartphones), medium screens (e.g., tablets), and large screens (e.g., desktops).

```css
/* Styles for small screens (less than 768px wide) */
@media (max-width: 768px) {
    /* CSS rules for small screens */
}

/* Styles for medium screens (between 768px and 1024px wide) */
@media (min-width: 769px) and (max-width: 1024px) {
    /* CSS rules for medium screens */
}

/* Styles for large screens (greater than 1024px wide) */
@media (min-width: 1025px) {
    /* CSS rules for large screens */
}
```

Orientation-Based Media Queries

You can also use media queries to apply styles based on the orientation of the device. For instance, you may want to adjust styles when a device switches from portrait to landscape mode.

```css
/* Styles for devices in portrait mode */
@media (orientation: portrait) {
    /* CSS rules for portrait orientation */
}

/* Styles for devices in landscape mode */
@media (orientation: landscape) {
    /* CSS rules for landscape orientation */
}
```

High-Resolution Displays

To optimize your website for high-resolution screens like Retina displays, you can use media queries to serve higher-quality images or adjust font sizes.

```css
/* Styles for high-resolution displays (2x pixel density) */
@media (-webkit-min-device-pixel-ratio: 2), (min-resolution: 192dpi) {
    /* CSS rules for high-resolution displays */
}
```

Testing is crucial when working with media queries to ensure that your styles behave as expected on different devices. Most modern web browsers provide developer tools that allow you to simulate various screen sizes and orientations for testing.

In summary, media queries are a powerful tool for creating responsive web designs that adapt to different devices and screen sizes. By using them effectively, you can provide a seamless and user-friendly experience across the wide range of devices used to access the web today.

Section 10.3: Fluid Layouts and Flexible Images

In responsive web design, creating fluid layouts and ensuring that images adapt to different screen sizes are essential practices. Fluid layouts allow your web content to expand or contract based on the viewport width, ensuring a consistent user experience across devices. Let's explore how to design fluid layouts and make images flexible in Section 10.3.

Designing Fluid Layouts

To create a fluid layout, you need to use relative units like percentages for widths and paddings instead of fixed pixel values. Here are some key concepts to consider:

1. **Percentage-Based Widths:** Instead of setting fixed pixel widths for elements, use percentages. For example, to create a two-column layout, you might set each column to be 50% wide.

   ```
   .column {
       width: 50%;
   }
   ```

2. **Max-Width:** While percentages can make elements fluid, you may want to set a `max-width` to prevent elements from becoming too wide on large screens. This ensures a better reading experience.

   ```
   .container {
       max-width: 1200px; /* Adjust as needed */
       margin: 0 auto; /* Center the container */
   }
   ```

3. **Flexible Margins and Padding:** Use percentages for margins and padding to maintain consistent spacing relative to the element's width.

   ```
   .box {
       padding: 5%;
   }
   ```

4. **Media Queries:** Combine fluid layouts with media queries to adjust the layout at different screen widths, providing the best user experience for various devices.

```
/* Styles for screens less than 768px wide */
@media (max-width: 768px) {
    .column {
        width: 100%; /* Full-width on small screens */
    }
}
```

Making Images Flexible

Images play a crucial role in responsive design. You want them to scale appropriately without losing quality or causing layout issues. Here's how to make images responsive:

1. **Max-Width for Images:** Set a max-width: 100% on images to ensure they don't exceed the width of their container. This prevents images from overflowing and breaking the layout.

```
img {
    max-width: 100%;
    height: auto;
}
```

2. **Retina-Ready Images:** To serve high-quality images to high-resolution screens, you can use CSS media queries to apply different image sources based on screen density.

```
/* For high-resolution screens */
@media (-webkit-min-device-pixel-ratio: 2), (min-resolution: 192dpi) {
    img {
        background-image: url('image@2x.jpg');
    }
}
```

3. **Images as Backgrounds:** When using images as backgrounds for elements, you can set background properties like background-size to control how they scale.

```
.header {
    background-image: url('header-image.jpg');
    background-size: cover; /* Cover the entire container */
    background-position: center center; /* Center the image */
}
```

By implementing fluid layouts and ensuring that images scale gracefully, you can create responsive web designs that adapt seamlessly to different screen sizes and resolutions. These techniques enhance user experience and make your website accessible across a wide range of devices.

Section 10.4: Mobile-First Design Approach

In Section 10.4, we'll explore the mobile-first design approach, a fundamental principle of responsive web design. Mobile-first design prioritizes the development of a website's mobile version before addressing larger screens. This approach ensures that your site functions well on small screens and progressively enhances the user experience on larger devices.

Why Mobile-First?

Mobile devices have become the primary means of accessing the internet. Designing for mobile-first offers several advantages:

1. **Performance:** Mobile-first design encourages optimizing performance for smaller devices, resulting in faster load times and a better user experience.

2. **Content Focus:** Starting with a mobile design forces you to prioritize essential content, ensuring that users on all devices get the most critical information.

3. **Progressive Enhancement:** Building a mobile-first design provides a solid foundation. As screen sizes increase, you can add enhancements and additional features.

4. **SEO Benefits:** Google and other search engines prioritize mobile-friendly websites in search results, making mobile-first design critical for SEO.

Key Mobile-First Principles

To implement a mobile-first design approach effectively, consider these principles:

1. **Start with a Narrow Viewport:** Begin the design process with the smallest screen size in mind, typically smartphones. This forces you to focus on essential content and functionality.

2. **Responsive Design:** Use responsive design techniques like media queries to adapt the layout and content as the screen size increases. This ensures your site looks good on both small and large screens.

   ```
   /* Example media query for screens larger than 768px */
   @media (min-width: 769px) {
       /* CSS rules for larger screens go here */
   }
   ```

3. **Fluid Layouts:** Create flexible, fluid layouts that adjust to different screen sizes. Use relative units like percentages and ems for element sizing.

   ```
   .container {
       max-width: 100%;
   ```

```
    padding: 2%;
}
```

4. **Progressive Enhancement:** Add additional features, content, and interactions for larger screens. Avoid overloading mobile users with unnecessary elements.

5. **Optimize Performance:** Pay attention to performance optimization, such as image compression and lazy loading, to ensure fast loading times on mobile devices.

6. **User Testing:** Test your mobile design on actual devices or using mobile emulators to identify and fix usability issues.

7. **Accessibility:** Ensure that your mobile design is accessible to users with disabilities by following accessibility guidelines.

Implementation

To implement a mobile-first design, start by creating the mobile layout using CSS media queries for larger screens. Here's a simplified example:

```css
/* Base styles for mobile */
.header {
    background-color: #333;
    color: #fff;
    padding: 10px;
    text-align: center;
}

/* Styles for screens larger than 768px */
@media (min-width: 769px) {
    .header {
        padding: 20px;
    }
}
```

By embracing the mobile-first design philosophy, you can deliver an optimal user experience to all visitors, regardless of their device. This approach ensures that your website is future-proof and adapts to evolving technology and user habits.

Section 10.5: Testing and Debugging Responsive Sites

In Section 10.5, we will discuss the importance of testing and debugging responsive websites. Building a responsive web design is crucial to ensure that your site looks and functions well on various devices and screen sizes. However, achieving a flawless responsive design can be challenging, and issues may arise during development. This section will guide you through the best practices for testing and debugging responsive sites effectively.

Why Test and Debug Responsive Sites?

Testing and debugging responsive websites are essential for the following reasons:

1. **Cross-Device Compatibility:** Your website should work seamlessly across a wide range of devices, including smartphones, tablets, laptops, and desktop computers.

2. **User Experience:** Responsive design directly impacts user experience. A site that doesn't adapt to different screens can frustrate visitors and lead to high bounce rates.

3. **SEO Ranking:** Search engines like Google prioritize mobile-friendly websites. A poorly responsive site can affect your search engine rankings.

Testing Tools and Techniques

To ensure your responsive design functions as intended, use the following testing tools and techniques:

1. **Device Emulators:** Emulators simulate different devices, allowing you to view your site as it appears on smartphones, tablets, and other devices. Popular options include Chrome DevTools' device mode and online emulators like BrowserStack and Responsinator.

2. **Viewport Testing:** Manually resize your browser window to various widths to observe how your design adapts. Pay attention to the layout, text readability, and image scaling.

3. **Browser Testing:** Test your site on various web browsers (e.g., Chrome, Firefox, Safari, Edge) to identify any compatibility issues. Browser-specific CSS and JavaScript may be required for optimal performance.

4. **Mobile Testing:** Test on real mobile devices whenever possible. This provides the most accurate representation of how your site performs on smartphones and tablets.

Debugging Common Issues

When testing reveals issues in your responsive design, you can debug the following common problems:

1. **Layout Breaks:** Elements overlapping or breaking out of their containers can occur when CSS rules conflict or when the layout isn't fluid enough. Use CSS debugging tools like browser DevTools to inspect and modify styles.

2. **Media Queries:** Ensure that your media queries trigger correctly at specific breakpoints. Check for syntax errors and conflicting styles.

3. **Image Optimization:** Images may not load or display correctly on mobile devices. Use responsive image techniques like `max-width: 100%` to prevent images from exceeding their container's width.

4. **Touchscreen Interactions:** Test touchscreen-specific interactions, such as touch gestures and swipes, on mobile devices to ensure smooth navigation.

5. **Performance Issues:** Monitor your site's performance on various devices using tools like Google PageSpeed Insights and GTmetrix. Optimize images, scripts, and CSS to improve load times.

6. **Content Readability:** Verify that text remains readable and legible on small screens. Adjust font sizes and line spacing if necessary.

7. **Accessibility:** Test your site's accessibility using tools like WAVE or Axe to ensure it complies with web accessibility standards (WCAG).

Version Control and Backups

Before making significant changes during debugging, ensure you have a version control system in place (e.g., Git) and backups of your website. This safeguards your progress and allows you to revert to a previous state if needed.

In conclusion, thorough testing and effective debugging are crucial steps in achieving a responsive web design that provides an excellent user experience on all devices. Regularly update and test your site to adapt to evolving technologies and user expectations.

Chapter 11: CSS Frameworks and Libraries

Section 11.1: Introduction to CSS Frameworks

In the world of web design and development, CSS (Cascading Style Sheets) frameworks have become valuable tools for creating responsive and visually appealing websites more efficiently. CSS frameworks provide a pre-built collection of CSS rules, styles, and components that can be easily integrated into your web projects. They are particularly beneficial for streamlining the design process and ensuring cross-browser compatibility. In this section, we will explore the fundamentals of CSS frameworks and how they can enhance your web design workflow.

What Are CSS Frameworks?

CSS frameworks are sets of pre-designed CSS files, often accompanied by JavaScript components, that aim to simplify the process of styling web pages. They offer a consistent and structured approach to styling web elements, making it easier for developers to create responsive and visually appealing layouts.

Advantages of Using CSS Frameworks

1. **Rapid Development**: CSS frameworks provide a starting point with pre-defined styles, grids, and components, reducing the need to write extensive custom CSS from scratch. This accelerates development.

2. **Consistency**: Frameworks ensure a consistent design across your website, making it easier to maintain and update styles as needed.

3. **Responsive Design**: Many CSS frameworks come with responsive grids and components, helping you create mobile-friendly layouts effortlessly.

4. **Cross-Browser Compatibility**: CSS frameworks are rigorously tested across different browsers, ensuring that your website looks and functions consistently across various platforms.

5. **Community Support**: Popular frameworks have active communities, offering documentation, tutorials, and third-party plugins to extend functionality.

Popular CSS Frameworks

1. **Bootstrap**: Bootstrap is one of the most widely used CSS frameworks. It offers a comprehensive set of responsive design components, such as navigation bars, buttons, forms, and grids.

2. **Foundation**: Foundation is known for its flexibility and scalability. It provides a modular approach to design, allowing you to pick and choose the components you need.

3. **Bulma**: Bulma is a lightweight and modern CSS framework that focuses on simplicity and ease of use. It's a great choice for projects that require a minimalist design.

4. **Semantic UI**: Semantic UI emphasizes human-friendly HTML and intuitive classes. It encourages semantic HTML while providing visually appealing styles.

Getting Started with a CSS Framework

To start using a CSS framework, you typically include the framework's CSS and JavaScript files in your HTML document. You can then apply the framework's classes to your HTML elements to achieve the desired styling and layout. Each framework has its own documentation, which provides detailed instructions on how to use its components effectively.

Conclusion

CSS frameworks are valuable resources for web designers and developers looking to streamline their workflow and create visually appealing, responsive websites. In the next sections, we will dive deeper into specific CSS frameworks and explore their features in more detail.

Section 11.2: Using Bootstrap for Responsive Design

Bootstrap is a popular CSS framework developed by Twitter, and it has gained widespread adoption in the web development community. In this section, we will explore the key features and usage of Bootstrap for creating responsive and visually appealing web designs.

Getting Started with Bootstrap

To use Bootstrap in your web project, you can either download it from the official Bootstrap website or include it via a Content Delivery Network (CDN). Including Bootstrap via a CDN is a convenient way to get started quickly, as it doesn't require downloading and hosting the framework files on your server.

Here's how to include Bootstrap via a CDN in your HTML document:

```
<!DOCTYPE html>
<html lang="en">
<head>
    <meta charset="UTF-8">
    <meta name="viewport" content="width=device-width, initial-scale=1.0">
    <title>Bootstrap Example</title>

    <!-- Include Bootstrap CSS via CDN -->
    <link rel="stylesheet"
href="https://cdn.jsdelivr.net/npm/bootstrap@5.3.0/dist/css/bootstrap.min.css
```

```
">
</head>
<body>
    <!-- Your Bootstrap-based content goes here -->

    <!-- Include Bootstrap JavaScript via CDN (optional) -->
    <script
src="https://cdn.jsdelivr.net/npm/bootstrap@5.3.0/dist/js/bootstrap.min.js"><
/script>
</body>
</html>
```

Grid System

One of Bootstrap's standout features is its responsive grid system. It allows you to create complex layouts that adapt to different screen sizes, making your website look great on both desktop and mobile devices.

Here's an example of a simple Bootstrap grid layout:

```
<div class="container">
    <div class="row">
        <div class="col-md-6">
            <!-- Content for the left column -->
        </div>
        <div class="col-md-6">
            <!-- Content for the right column -->
        </div>
    </div>
</div>
```

In this example, the `container` class creates a container with a responsive width, and the `row` class defines a row within that container. Within the row, you can use `col-md-*` classes to specify the number of columns each element should occupy, based on the screen size.

Responsive Navigation Bar

Bootstrap provides a responsive navigation bar component that adapts to different screen sizes. Here's an example of a simple Bootstrap navbar:

```
<nav class="navbar navbar-expand-lg navbar-light bg-light">
    <a class="navbar-brand" href="#">My Website</a>
    <button class="navbar-toggler" type="button" data-toggle="collapse" data-
target="#navbarNav" aria-controls="navbarNav" aria-expanded="false" aria-
label="Toggle navigation">
        <span class="navbar-toggler-icon"></span>
    </button>
    <div class="collapse navbar-collapse" id="navbarNav">
        <ul class="navbar-nav ml-auto">
            <li class="nav-item active">
                <a class="nav-link" href="#">Home</a>
```

```
            </li>
            <li class="nav-item">
                <a class="nav-link" href="#">About</a>
            </li>
            <li class="nav-item">
                <a class="nav-link" href="#">Services</a>
            </li>
            <li class="nav-item">
                <a class="nav-link" href="#">Contact</a>
            </li>
        </ul>
    </div>
</nav>
```

This code creates a responsive navigation bar with a collapsible menu for smaller screens.

CSS Classes and Components

Bootstrap provides a wide range of CSS classes and pre-designed components like buttons, forms, alerts, and modals that you can easily incorporate into your project. By applying Bootstrap classes to your HTML elements, you can achieve consistent styling and layout.

Customization

Bootstrap is highly customizable. You can use its extensive set of variables and themes to customize the look and feel of your website to match your brand. Additionally, you can choose to include only the Bootstrap components that you need to optimize performance.

Conclusion

Bootstrap is a versatile CSS framework that simplifies responsive web design and offers a wide array of components and utilities. In the next sections, we will explore more Bootstrap features and demonstrate how to use them effectively in your web projects.

Section 11.3: CSS Grid Systems

CSS grid systems are a fundamental part of web design, enabling the creation of flexible and responsive layouts. In this section, we will delve into CSS grid systems, how they work, and how you can utilize them in your web development projects.

Understanding CSS Grid

CSS Grid is a layout system that allows you to divide a web page into a grid of rows and columns, making it easy to arrange content. It provides precise control over the placement and sizing of elements within the grid, making it a powerful tool for responsive web design.

To create a grid container, you can use the display: grid; property in CSS. For example:

```
.grid-container {
    display: grid;
    grid-template-columns: repeat(3, 1fr);
    grid-gap: 20px;
}
```

In this example, we've created a grid container with three columns of equal width and a gap of 20 pixels between grid items.

Defining Grid Rows and Columns

You can define the rows and columns of your grid using various properties like grid-template-columns and grid-template-rows. These properties allow you to specify the size and behavior of the grid tracks.

Here's an example of defining a grid with two rows and three columns:

```
.grid-container {
    display: grid;
    grid-template-columns: repeat(3, 1fr);
    grid-template-rows: 100px 200px;
}
```

In this example, we have two rows with heights of 100 pixels and 200 pixels, respectively.

Placing Grid Items

To place items within the grid, you can use the grid-column and grid-row properties. For example:

```
.grid-item {
    grid-column: 2 / 4; /* Start at column 2 and end at column 4 */
    grid-row: 1 / span 2; /* Start at row 1 and span 2 rows */
}
```

This code places a grid item that starts at the second column and ends at the fourth column, while also spanning two rows.

Grid Item Auto Placement

CSS Grid also supports automatic placement of grid items using the grid-auto-flow property. By default, it places items in rows, but you can change this behavior to columns if needed.

```
.grid-container {
    display: grid;
    grid-template-columns: repeat(3, 1fr);
    grid-auto-flow: column; /* Automatically place items in columns */
}
```

Responsive Grids

CSS Grid is particularly useful for responsive web design. You can use media queries to adjust the grid layout based on the screen size. This ensures that your web page looks great on various devices, from desktops to smartphones.

```css
@media screen and (max-width: 768px) {
  .grid-container {
    grid-template-columns: 1fr; /* Single column layout for smaller screens */
  }
}
```

Conclusion

CSS Grid is a powerful tool for creating flexible and responsive layouts in web design. Understanding how to define grids, place items, and use media queries to adapt to different screen sizes is essential for modern web development. In the following sections, we will explore more layout techniques and frameworks to enhance your web design skills.

Section 11.4: Customizing Frameworks

While CSS frameworks like Bootstrap and Foundation provide pre-designed components and layouts, there are times when you need more customized styles to match your project's unique requirements. In this section, we'll explore how to customize CSS frameworks and make them align with your specific design vision.

Why Customize a CSS Framework?

CSS frameworks are designed to be flexible and adaptable, but they often come with their default styles and components. Customizing a CSS framework allows you to:

1. **Achieve a Unique Look**: Customize the framework to create a design that stands out and aligns with your brand or project's aesthetic.

2. **Optimize for Performance**: Remove unnecessary styles and components to reduce the CSS file size, improving page load times.

3. **Meet Project Requirements**: Tailor the framework to meet specific project requirements that might not be covered by the default styles.

Steps to Customize a CSS Framework

1. **Import the Framework**: Begin by importing the CSS framework into your project. You can usually do this by linking to the framework's stylesheet in your HTML file.

2. **Create a Custom Stylesheet**: To customize the framework, create a new CSS file for your custom styles. This file will override the framework's default styles.

3. **Inspect and Override Styles**: Use browser developer tools to inspect the elements you want to customize. Identify the CSS classes or IDs associated with those elements and override them in your custom stylesheet.

```css
/* Example: Changing the background color of a button */
.btn-primary {
    background-color: #ff5733;
}
```

4. **Organize Your Custom Styles**: Maintain a clear and organized structure for your custom stylesheet. Group styles by components or sections to keep things manageable.

5. **Testing and Iteration**: Continuously test your custom styles on different devices and screen sizes. Make adjustments as needed to ensure a responsive and consistent design.

Customization Examples

Here are a few common customization examples:

1. Modifying Typography

You can customize fonts, font sizes, line heights, and text colors to match your design's typography.

```css
/* Example: Changing the font family and size for headings */
h1, h2, h3 {
    font-family: "Arial", sans-serif;
    font-size: 28px;
    color: #333;
}
```

2. Adjusting Colors

Customize the color scheme of the framework to match your brand's colors.

```css
/* Example: Changing the primary and secondary colors */
.btn-primary {
    background-color: #ff5733;
    border-color: #ff5733;
    color: #fff;
}
```

3. Customizing Buttons

Tailor button styles to fit your design's button hierarchy and size requirements.

```css
/* Example: Customizing button sizes */
.btn-large {
    font-size: 20px;
    padding: 10px 20px;
}
```

```
}
.btn-small {
  font-size: 14px;
  padding: 5px 10px;
}
```

Conclusion

Customizing a CSS framework allows you to retain the benefits of a responsive and well-tested design system while tailoring it to your specific needs. Whether it's adjusting colors, typography, or component styles, customization ensures that your web project has a unique and polished look that aligns with your goals. Remember to document your custom styles for consistency and ease of maintenance as your project evolves.

Section 11.5: Integrating External Libraries

In modern web development, it's common to leverage external libraries and plugins to enhance the functionality and features of your website or web application. These libraries provide pre-built solutions for various tasks, saving you development time and effort. In this section, we'll explore the process of integrating external libraries into your web projects.

Selecting the Right Library

Before integrating an external library, it's essential to choose the right one for your project. Consider the following factors:

1. **Compatibility**: Ensure that the library is compatible with your existing technology stack, including your CSS framework, JavaScript framework, and other dependencies.

2. **Documentation**: Check the library's documentation to understand its features, usage, and customization options. Well-documented libraries are easier to work with.

3. **Community Support**: Libraries with an active community are more likely to receive updates, bug fixes, and support from other developers.

4. **Performance**: Evaluate the library's impact on your website's performance. Some libraries might add significant overhead to your page load times.

5. **License**: Be aware of the library's license. Some libraries may have usage restrictions or require attribution.

Adding External Libraries

Once you've chosen a library, follow these general steps to integrate it into your project:

1. **Download or Include via CDN**: Libraries can be included in your project by downloading the library files and hosting them locally or by linking to them via a Content Delivery Network (CDN). Using a CDN is convenient for widely-used libraries like jQuery or Font Awesome.

    ```
    <!-- Example: Including jQuery via CDN -->
    <script src="https://code.jquery.com/jquery-3.6.0.min.js"></script>
    ```

2. **Include Scripts and Stylesheets**: Add the library's JavaScript and CSS files to your HTML document. Ensure that the order of inclusion is correct, especially when scripts depend on other scripts.

    ```
    <!-- Example: Including a library's JavaScript and CSS -->
    <link rel="stylesheet" href="library.css">
    <script src="library.js"></script>
    ```

3. **Initialization**: Initialize and configure the library as needed. This often involves calling specific functions or methods provided by the library.

    ```
    // Example: Initializing a carousel plugin
    $(document).ready(function() {
      $('.carousel').carousel();
    });
    ```

4. **Customization**: Customize the library's behavior and appearance to match your project's requirements. This may involve modifying configuration options or overriding default styles.

    ```
    // Example: Customizing a date picker library
    $('#date-input').datepicker({
      format: 'dd/mm/yyyy',
      autoclose: true
    });
    ```

5. **Testing and Debugging**: Thoroughly test the library's integration, ensuring it functions correctly on different devices and browsers. Use browser developer tools to debug any issues that arise.

6. **Documentation and Maintenance**: Document the usage of the library within your project for future reference. Keep an eye on updates and security patches provided by the library's maintainers.

Common External Libraries

There are numerous external libraries available for various purposes. Here are some common categories of libraries you may consider integrating:

-   **JavaScript Frameworks and Libraries**: Libraries like jQuery, React, and Vue.js for building interactive web applications.

- **UI Component Libraries**: Framework-agnostic UI component libraries like Material-UI, Ant Design, or Bootstrap that provide pre-designed user interface elements.

- **Charting and Data Visualization Libraries**: Libraries like Chart.js and D3.js for creating interactive charts and graphs.

- **Animation Libraries**: Libraries like GreenSock Animation Platform (GSAP) for creating animations and transitions.

- **Form Validation Libraries**: Libraries like Parsley.js for client-side form validation.

- **Rich Text Editors**: Libraries like TinyMCE and CKEditor for implementing rich text editors in web forms.

- **Mapping and Geolocation Libraries**: Libraries like Leaflet and Google Maps API for adding maps and location-based features.

Conclusion

Integrating external libraries into your web projects can significantly extend your site's capabilities and save development time. However, it's crucial to choose libraries carefully, follow best practices for integration, and stay informed about updates and security issues. By doing so, you can leverage the power of the broader web development community to enhance your projects.

Chapter 12: Web Typography

Section 12.1: Typography Fundamentals

Typography plays a crucial role in web design, as it directly affects how users perceive and interact with your content. In this section, we'll explore the fundamentals of typography and how to make informed decisions about fonts, spacing, and readability in your web projects.

The Anatomy of Typography

Typography involves a range of elements that contribute to the overall visual and textual experience. Here are some key components:

1. **Font**: A font is a specific design of a set of characters, including letters, numbers, and symbols. Fonts can convey different moods and styles, so selecting the right font is essential.

2. **Typeface**: A typeface refers to a family of fonts that share a similar design style. For example, Arial and Helvetica are different fonts within the same sans-serif typeface.

3. **Font Size**: Font size determines how large or small text appears on a web page. It's typically measured in points (pt) or pixels (px) and affects readability.

4. **Line Height**: Line height, also known as leading, is the vertical space between lines of text. Proper line height improves readability and prevents text from appearing cramped.

5. **Character Spacing**: Character spacing, also called tracking or letter spacing, adjusts the space between individual characters. It can affect readability and the overall visual appeal.

6. **Text Alignment**: Text can be aligned left, right, center, or justified. Alignment choices impact the way users read and engage with content.

7. **Typography Hierarchy**: Establishing a hierarchy of fonts and font sizes helps emphasize different parts of your content. For instance, headings are typically larger and bolder than body text.

Font Categories

Fonts are categorized based on their design characteristics, and each category serves a specific purpose. Here are some common font categories:

- **Serif Fonts**: Serif fonts have small decorative lines at the ends of characters. They are often associated with tradition, formality, and print media. Examples include Times New Roman and Georgia.

- **Sans-Serif Fonts**: Sans-serif fonts lack the decorative lines (serifs) and have a clean, modern appearance. They are widely used in digital interfaces and convey simplicity and readability. Examples include Arial, Helvetica, and Open Sans.

- **Monospace Fonts**: Monospace fonts have equal spacing between characters, making them ideal for code and tabular data. Each character occupies the same horizontal space. Examples include Courier New and Consolas.

- **Display Fonts**: Display fonts are decorative and eye-catching. They are used for headlines and logos but should be used sparingly for body text due to reduced readability. Examples include Lobster and Pacifico.

- **Script Fonts**: Script fonts mimic handwriting and add a personal touch to designs. They are often used for invitations and artistic projects. Examples include Brush Script and Great Vibes.

Readability and Legibility

Readability refers to how easily text can be read, while legibility focuses on how well individual characters can be distinguished. Both are crucial for effective communication on the web.

To improve readability and legibility:

- Use appropriate font sizes for different text elements. Body text should typically be around 16-18px for optimal readability.

- Ensure sufficient contrast between text and background colors to avoid strain on the eyes.

- Maintain proper line height to prevent text from appearing cramped or too spaced out.

- Choose fonts and styles that match the tone and purpose of your content.

- Test your typography choices on various devices and screen sizes to ensure consistency and accessibility.

Web Typography Tools

There are various web typography tools and resources available to help you choose and implement fonts effectively:

- **Google Fonts**: Offers a vast collection of web fonts that you can easily integrate into your projects.

- **Adobe Fonts**: Provides access to high-quality fonts, and it's available to Adobe Creative Cloud subscribers.

- **Typekit**: Adobe's web font service, now integrated into Adobe Fonts, allows you to choose and use fonts for web design.

- **Font Squirrel**: Offers a collection of free fonts for commercial use and provides web font generator tools.

- **Font Awesome**: A popular icon font library that allows you to include scalable vector icons in your web projects.

Conclusion

Understanding the fundamentals of typography is essential for creating visually appealing and readable web designs. Carefully selecting fonts, considering font categories, and paying attention to readability and legibility contribute to a positive user experience. In the next sections, we'll explore web fonts and techniques for implementing them in your projects.

Section 12.2: Web Fonts and @font-face

Web fonts play a crucial role in web typography, allowing designers to use a wide range of fonts that may not be available on users' devices. In this section, we'll explore how to use web fonts effectively in your web design projects, including the @font-face rule and services like Google Fonts.

The Need for Web Fonts

While web browsers come with a default set of fonts, they are limited in number and style. To achieve unique and visually appealing typography in your web designs, you often need to use custom fonts that aren't available by default. This is where web fonts come into play.

Web fonts are font files hosted on a server and loaded into a web page when it is accessed by a user. They provide a consistent and accessible way to display custom fonts across various devices and browsers.

The @font-face Rule

The @font-face rule is a fundamental part of web font implementation. It allows you to specify custom fonts and provide the browser with the necessary font files. Here's a basic example of how to use @font-face:

```
@font-face {
  font-family: 'CustomFont';
  src: url('customfont.woff2') format('woff2'),
       url('customfont.woff') format('woff');
}
```

- font-family: This property defines the name of the custom font family, which you can use in your CSS to apply the font to specific elements.

- **src**: Here, you specify the file paths to the font files. It's a good practice to provide multiple formats (e.g., WOFF and WOFF2) to ensure compatibility across different browsers.

Once you've defined the `@font-face` rule, you can use the specified font-family in your CSS like this:

```css
body {
    font-family: 'CustomFont', sans-serif;
}
```

Web Font Services

Several web font services simplify the process of using custom fonts in your web projects. One of the most popular services is Google Fonts:

Google Fonts

Google Fonts offers a vast collection of open-source fonts that you can easily integrate into your websites. Here's how to use Google Fonts:

1. Visit the Google Fonts website and browse or search for the fonts you want to use.

2. Select the fonts you want to use by clicking the "+" icon next to each font.

3. After you've made your selections, click the "Family Selected" button at the bottom of the page.

4. In the pop-up window, you'll find the `<link>` tag that you need to include in the `<head>` section of your HTML file. It looks something like this:

```html
<link rel="stylesheet"
href="https://fonts.googleapis.com/css?family=Open+Sans">
```

5. Finally, apply the font to your CSS just like any other font family:

```css
body {
    font-family: 'Open Sans', sans-serif;
}
```

Font Loading Strategies

To optimize the performance of your web pages, you can implement font loading strategies. These techniques ensure that the most critical content is displayed while fonts are still loading. Some common strategies include:

- **Font Display Swap**: This strategy displays the fallback font until the custom font is fully loaded. To use it, modify your `<link>` tag like this:

```html
<link rel="stylesheet"
href="https://fonts.googleapis.com/css?family=Open+Sans&display=swap">
```

- **Font Loading API**: The Font Loading API provides more control over when and how fonts are loaded. You can use JavaScript to trigger font loading and apply fonts when they are available.

Conclusion

Web fonts and the @font-face rule are powerful tools for enhancing the typography of your web designs. Whether you're using custom fonts hosted on your server or relying on web font services like Google Fonts, careful implementation and consideration of font loading strategies can improve user experience and ensure that your text content is both stylish and accessible. In the next section, we'll explore font styling and effects to further enhance your typography.

Section 12.3: Font Styling and Effects

Typography is a fundamental aspect of web design, and how you style and enhance your text can greatly impact the overall look and feel of your website. In this section, we'll delve into various font styling and text effects that you can apply to your web typography to create visually engaging content.

Font Styling Properties

font-weight

The font-weight property allows you to control the thickness or boldness of a font. You can set it to values like normal, bold, bolder, or use numeric values like 100 (thin) to 900 (extra bold).

```
p {
    font-weight: bold;
}
```

font-style

The font-style property lets you set the style of the font, such as normal, italic, or oblique. Italicized fonts can provide emphasis and variation in your text.

```
em {
    font-style: italic;
}
```

text-transform

The text-transform property changes the capitalization of text. You can use values like uppercase, lowercase, or capitalize to modify how text is displayed.

```
h2 {
    text-transform: uppercase;
}
```

text-decoration

To add decorative elements to text, you can use the `text-decoration` property. Common values include `underline`, `overline`, `line-through`, or a combination.

```
a:hover {
    text-decoration: underline;
}
```

Text Shadows

Adding shadows to text can create depth and make it stand out. Use the `text-shadow` property to apply a shadow to your text.

```
h3 {
    text-shadow: 2px 2px 4px rgba(0, 0, 0, 0.5);
}
```

- The first value represents the horizontal offset of the shadow.
- The second value represents the vertical offset.
- The third value is the blur radius of the shadow.
- The fourth value is the color of the shadow in `rgba` format.

Letter Spacing and Line Height

Adjusting the spacing between letters and lines can significantly impact readability and visual appeal.

letter-spacing

The `letter-spacing` property controls the space between characters in a text element. You can use this to create a tighter or looser text layout.

```
blockquote {
    letter-spacing: 2px;
}
```

line-height

The `line-height` property sets the height of a line of text. It's crucial for readability and can be used to create more open or compact text layouts.

```
p {
    line-height: 1.5;
}
```

Custom Fonts with Font Icons

Font icons are a popular way to add scalable and stylized icons to your web pages. Icon fonts like FontAwesome provide a wide range of icons that you can easily incorporate into your design.

```
<i class="fas fa-heart"></i> Like
<i class="fas fa-comment"></i> Comment
```

Conclusion

Styling and enhancing your web typography is essential for creating visually appealing and engaging content. By using properties like `font-weight`, `font-style`, `text-transform`, and `text-decoration`, you can control how text is displayed. Additionally, techniques such as adding text shadows, adjusting letter spacing, and managing line height contribute to improved aesthetics and readability.

In the next section, we'll explore the pairing of fonts for web design, helping you choose complementary typefaces that work well together to create harmonious and balanced typography.

Section 12.4: Pairing Fonts for Web Design

Choosing the right combination of fonts for your web design is a crucial aspect of typography. Well-paired fonts can enhance the readability, aesthetics, and overall appeal of your website. In this section, we'll explore principles and techniques for selecting and pairing fonts effectively.

Principles of Font Pairing

1. **Contrast**: Combining fonts with contrasting styles creates visual interest. Pair a serif font with a sans-serif font or a bold typeface with a lighter one.

2. **Consistency**: Maintain consistency in font pairing throughout your website to establish a cohesive and professional appearance.

3. **Hierarchy**: Use font pairing to establish a hierarchy of content. Headings may use a different font than body text to draw attention.

4. **Readability**: Prioritize readability. Ensure that the chosen fonts are legible on various screen sizes and devices.

Font Categories

Serif Fonts

Serif fonts have small decorative strokes at the end of characters. They are often associated with traditional and formal designs. Popular serif fonts include Times New Roman, Georgia, and Baskerville.

Sans-Serif Fonts

Sans-serif fonts lack decorative strokes and offer a clean and modern appearance. Common sans-serif fonts include Arial, Helvetica, and Open Sans.

Display fonts are decorative and eye-catching. They are suitable for headlines and logos but may not be ideal for body text due to reduced readability. Examples include Lobster and Pacifico.

Monospaced Fonts

Monospaced fonts have equal spacing between characters, making them suitable for code and technical content. Courier and Consolas are well-known monospaced fonts.

Font Pairing Techniques

1. **Serif with Sans-Serif**: Pair a serif font for headings with a sans-serif font for body text, creating a balanced contrast.

2. **Similar Fonts with Different Weights**: Use the same font family but vary the weights (e.g., regular and bold) for hierarchy and consistency.

3. **Complementary Fonts**: Choose fonts that complement each other in terms of style and mood. For example, pair a modern sans-serif with a vintage display font for a unique look.

4. **Size and Style Variations**: Adjust font sizes and styles to create a hierarchy. Use larger and bolder fonts for headings and smaller, regular fonts for body text.

Practical Font Pairing Examples

Example 1: Classic Combination

- Heading: **Playfair Display**
- Body Text: **Roboto**

```
h1 {
    font-family: 'Playfair Display', serif;
}

p {
    font-family: 'Roboto', sans-serif;
}
```

Example 2: Modern and Clean

- Heading: **Montserrat**
- Body Text: **Open Sans**

```
h1 {
    font-family: 'Montserrat', sans-serif;
}

p {
    font-family: 'Open Sans', sans-serif;
}
```

- Heading: **Cormorant Garamond**
- Body Text: **Lora**

```
h1 {
  font-family: 'Cormorant Garamond', serif;
}

p {
  font-family: 'Lora', serif;
}
```

Remember that the specific fonts you choose should align with your website's branding, content, and target audience. Experiment with different combinations to find the perfect pair that enhances your web design.

In the next section, we'll explore various typography tools and resources that can assist you in finding, managing, and implementing fonts effectively in your web projects.

Section 12.5: Typography Tools and Resources

Typography is a critical element of web design, and there are various tools and resources available to help you make informed decisions, manage fonts efficiently, and enhance your typographic skills. In this section, we'll explore some valuable typography tools and resources that can aid you in your web design journey.

Typography Tools

1. **Google Fonts**: Google Fonts offers a vast collection of web fonts that you can easily embed into your web projects. You can browse, preview, and select fonts suitable for your website's style.

2. **Adobe Fonts**: Adobe Fonts (formerly Typekit) provides access to a wide range of high-quality fonts that sync directly with Adobe Creative Cloud applications, making it convenient for designers.

3. **Type Scale**: Type Scale is a simple online tool that helps you create harmonious typography by generating a consistent scale of font sizes based on a selected ratio.

4. **Font Pairing Tools**: Tools like Fontjoy and Typ.io offer font pairing suggestions and examples, helping you find complementary fonts for your designs.

5. **WhatTheFont**: If you come across a font you'd like to identify, WhatTheFont allows you to upload an image containing the font, and it will attempt to identify it.

1. **Typography Books**: Books like "The Elements of Typographic Style" by Robert Bringhurst and "Thinking with Type" by Ellen Lupton are excellent resources for in-depth typographic knowledge.

2. **Online Typography Courses**: Websites like Coursera and Udemy offer courses on typography, taught by industry professionals, allowing you to deepen your typographic skills.

3. **Typography Blogs**: Blogs like "Typewolf" and "I Love Typography" provide inspiration, font recommendations, and articles on typography trends.

4. **Typography Forums**: Platforms like Typophile and TypeDrawers are communities where typography enthusiasts and professionals discuss type-related topics and seek advice.

5. **Typography Cheat Sheets**: Printable typography cheat sheets are available online, summarizing key typographic principles, terminology, and keyboard shortcuts.

Font Management Software

Efficient font management is crucial when working with multiple fonts in web design. Consider using font management software like:

1. **Adobe Font Manager**: Integrated with Adobe Creative Cloud apps, it allows you to activate and deactivate fonts as needed.

2. **FontBase**: A free font manager with features for browsing, organizing, and activating fonts, compatible with Windows, macOS, and Linux.

3. **FontExplorer X**: A professional font management tool that offers font activation, organization, and collaboration features.

4. **Suitcase Fusion**: A font manager with auto-activation, font organization, and cloud-based font sharing capabilities.

Design Inspiration

Exploring web design galleries and portfolios can provide inspiration for typography choices. Websites like Awwwards and Behance showcase outstanding web designs that often include innovative typography.

As you continue your web design journey, remember that typography plays a significant role in user experience and branding. The right fonts and typographic choices can elevate your design and convey your message effectively. Utilize these tools and resources to enhance your typographic skills and create visually appealing web experiences.

Chapter 13: Multimedia Integration

Multimedia integration is a fundamental aspect of web design that allows you to incorporate various types of media, such as images, audio, and video, into your web pages. This chapter explores the key considerations, techniques, and best practices for effectively working with multimedia elements to enhance the user experience.

Section 13.1: Working with Images and Graphics

Images and graphics are essential elements of web design, contributing to the visual appeal and engagement of a website. Here, we'll delve into the various aspects of working with images and graphics in web design.

Image Formats

When using images on your website, it's crucial to choose the appropriate image format. The most common image formats for the web include:

- **JPEG (Joint Photographic Experts Group)**: Ideal for photographs and images with many colors. JPEGs use lossy compression, which reduces file size but may impact image quality.

- **PNG (Portable Network Graphics)**: Suitable for images with transparency or sharp edges, like logos and icons. PNGs use lossless compression, preserving image quality.

- **GIF (Graphics Interchange Format)**: Often used for simple animations and small graphics. GIFs support transparency and have a limited color palette.

- **SVG (Scalable Vector Graphics)**: Best for vector graphics and logos that need to scale without losing quality. SVGs are XML-based and can be manipulated with CSS and JavaScript.

Image Optimization

To ensure fast-loading web pages, it's essential to optimize images for the web. Optimization techniques include:

- **Resizing**: Use image editing software to resize images to the dimensions required for your website, avoiding unnecessarily large files.

- **Compression**: Compress images to reduce file size. Tools like Photoshop, ImageOptim, and TinyPNG can help with this.

- **Lazy Loading**: Implement lazy loading to load images only when they are visible in the user's viewport, reducing initial page load times.

- **Responsive Images**: Use the `srcset` attribute to provide different image sizes for different screen resolutions and devices, improving performance on mobile devices.

Image Accessibility

Web accessibility is crucial, and images should be made accessible to users with disabilities. Here are some accessibility considerations:

- **Alt Text**: Always provide descriptive alt text for images. This text is read aloud by screen readers, allowing visually impaired users to understand the image's content and context.

- **Decorative Images**: Use empty or null alt text for purely decorative images that don't convey meaningful content. This tells screen readers to ignore them.

- **Image Descriptions**: For complex images that require detailed descriptions, consider using the `longdesc` attribute or providing additional information nearby.

Image Placement and Alignment

Consider the layout and placement of images within your web design:

- **Alignment**: Use CSS to control the alignment of images within text content. Common alignment options include left, right, and center.

- **Image Galleries**: When displaying multiple images, consider using image galleries or sliders to organize and present them in an engaging way.

Image Optimization Tools

Several tools can assist in optimizing and working with images:

- **Image Editing Software**: Tools like Adobe Photoshop, GIMP (GNU Image Manipulation Program), and Canva enable you to edit and manipulate images.

- **Image Compression Tools**: Online tools like TinyPNG, ImageOptim, and Compressor.io can help reduce image file sizes.

- **Image Sprites**: For icons and small graphics, consider creating image sprites, which combine multiple images into a single file to reduce server requests.

- **Image CDN (Content Delivery Network)**: CDNs like Cloudinary and Imgix can optimize, cache, and deliver images efficiently to users worldwide.

Working with images and graphics is a fundamental skill for web designers, as visual content plays a significant role in user engagement and storytelling. By understanding image formats, optimizing images for the web, ensuring accessibility, and using the right tools, you can create visually appealing and high-performing websites.

Section 13.2: Embedding Audio and Video

Multimedia elements like audio and video can greatly enrich the user experience on a website. In this section, we'll explore how to embed audio and video into web pages and consider best practices for ensuring compatibility and accessibility.

Embedding Audio

To embed audio on a web page, you can use the HTML <audio> element. Here's a basic example of how to embed an audio file:

```
<audio controls>
  <source src="audiofile.mp3" type="audio/mpeg">
  Your browser does not support the audio element.
</audio>
```

- The controls attribute adds audio playback controls (play, pause, volume) to the player.
- The <source> element specifies the audio file's source and its MIME type.

Audio File Formats

Different web browsers support various audio formats. To ensure compatibility, it's recommended to provide multiple source formats. Common audio formats for the web include MP3, Ogg Vorbis, and AAC. Here's an example with multiple sources:

```
<audio controls>
  <source src="audiofile.mp3" type="audio/mpeg">
  <source src="audiofile.ogg" type="audio/ogg">
  Your browser does not support the audio element.
</audio>
```

Audio Accessibility

To make audio content accessible, consider the following:

- Provide a descriptive text alternative using the <track> element for captions or transcripts.

```
<audio controls>
  <source src="audiofile.mp3" type="audio/mpeg">
  <track kind="captions" src="captions.vtt" srclang="en" label="English
Captions">
  Your browser does not support the audio element.
</audio>
```

- Ensure that audio controls are keyboard accessible and that users can navigate and operate them with screen readers.

Embedding Video

Embedding video on a web page is similar to audio and can be accomplished using the HTML <video> element. Here's a basic example:

```
<video controls>
  <source src="videofile.mp4" type="video/mp4">
  Your browser does not support the video element.
</video>
```

- The controls attribute adds video playback controls (play, pause, volume, fullscreen) to the player.
- The <source> element specifies the video file's source and its MIME type.

Video File Formats

Just like audio, different browsers support various video formats. Providing multiple source formats enhances compatibility. Common video formats include MP4, WebM, and Ogg.

```
<video controls>
  <source src="videofile.mp4" type="video/mp4">
  <source src="videofile.webm" type="video/webm">
  Your browser does not support the video element.
</video>
```

Video Accessibility

To make video content accessible:

- Use the <track> element for captions, subtitles, or transcripts.

```
<video controls>
  <source src="videofile.mp4" type="video/mp4">
  <track kind="captions" src="captions.vtt" srclang="en" label="English
Captions">
  Your browser does not support the video element.
</video>
```

- Ensure keyboard navigation and screen reader compatibility for video controls.

Responsive Multimedia

Consider the responsiveness of embedded multimedia elements by using CSS to control their dimensions and layout. This ensures that audio and video players adapt to different screen sizes and orientations.

```
/* Example CSS for responsive audio and video */
audio, video {
  max-width: 100%;
  height: auto;
}
```

By following these guidelines for embedding audio and video, you can create a more engaging and accessible web experience for your audience while ensuring compatibility across different web browsers.

Section 13.3: SVG Graphics for Scalability

Scalable Vector Graphics (SVG) is a widely used format for creating and displaying vector graphics on the web. Unlike raster graphics (e.g., JPEG or PNG), SVG graphics are resolution-independent, making them perfect for various screen sizes and resolutions. In this section, we'll explore SVG graphics, their advantages, and how to use them effectively in web design.

Advantages of SVG Graphics

1. **Resolution Independence**: SVG graphics are based on mathematical equations rather than pixels, ensuring they look crisp and clear on any screen, regardless of size or resolution.

2. **Small File Sizes**: SVG files are typically smaller than equivalent raster graphics, which can lead to faster loading times and reduced bandwidth usage.

3. **Scalability**: You can scale SVG graphics up or down without loss of quality. This is particularly useful for responsive web design, where elements need to adapt to various screen sizes.

4. **Editability**: SVG graphics are easy to edit using vector graphic software like Adobe Illustrator or open-source alternatives like Inkscape.

5. **Accessibility**: SVG graphics can be made accessible by adding text descriptions, making them usable for individuals with disabilities.

Creating SVG Graphics

You can create SVG graphics in several ways:

1. **Using Vector Graphic Software**: Tools like Adobe Illustrator, Inkscape, or CorelDRAW allow you to create complex SVG graphics.

2. **Online SVG Editors**: There are online SVG editors like SVG-Edit that provide a browser-based interface for creating and editing SVG graphics.

3. **Generating SVG with Code**: You can hand-code SVG graphics using plain text editors or integrated development environments (IDEs).

Here's a simple example of SVG code that draws a red circle:

```
<svg width="100" height="100" xmlns="http://www.w3.org/2000/svg">
  <circle cx="50" cy="50" r="40" fill="red" />
</svg>
```

Inline vs. External SVG

SVG graphics can be included in web pages in two ways: inline and external.

Inline SVG: This involves embedding the SVG code directly into your HTML document. Inline SVG is beneficial when you want to style or animate the graphic using CSS or JavaScript.

```
<svg width="100" height="100" xmlns="http://www.w3.org/2000/svg">
  <circle cx="50" cy="50" r="40" fill="blue" />
</svg>
```

External SVG: With this approach, you place the SVG code in a separate .svg file and reference it in your HTML. This is useful for reusing graphics across multiple pages or when working with larger, complex SVGs.

```
<svg width="100" height="100">
  <use xlink:href="graphic.svg#circle" />
</svg>
```

Styling SVG

You can style SVG graphics using CSS, just like any other HTML element. For example, you can change the color, stroke, or opacity of SVG shapes using CSS properties.

```
/* CSS for styling an SVG circle */
circle {
  fill: #ff9900; /* Change fill color to orange */
  stroke: #333; /* Add a black stroke */
  stroke-width: 2; /* Set the stroke width */
}
```

Animating SVG

SVG graphics can be animated using CSS animations or JavaScript libraries like GreenSock (GSAP). This allows for creating interactive and dynamic visuals on your web pages.

```
<svg width="100" height="100">
  <circle id="myCircle" cx="50" cy="50" r="40" fill="green" />
</svg>
```

```
/* CSS animation for scaling the circle */
@keyframes scaleAnimation {
  0% {
    transform: scale(1);
  }
  50% {
    transform: scale(1.2);
  }
  100% {
    transform: scale(1);
  }
```

```
}

#myCircle:hover {
  animation: scaleAnimation 1s infinite; /* Apply the animation on hover */
}
```

Optimizing SVG

To optimize SVG graphics for the web:

1. **Minimize Code**: Remove unnecessary attributes or elements to reduce file size.

2. **Compress**: Use online SVG optimizers or plugins to remove whitespace and compress the SVG code.

3. **Use viewBox**: Set the `viewBox` attribute to define the coordinate system and aspect ratio. This helps with responsive scaling.

Incorporating SVG graphics into your web design can enhance visual appeal, improve performance, and provide a scalable solution for various screen sizes. SVG's flexibility and adaptability make it a valuable tool for modern web design practices.

Section 13.4: Optimizing Multimedia for the Web

Multimedia elements like images, audio, and video are essential components of modern web design. However, they can significantly impact a website's performance if not optimized properly. In this section, we will explore various techniques for optimizing multimedia assets to ensure faster load times and a better user experience.

Image Optimization

Images are one of the most common multimedia elements on websites. Optimizing images is crucial for reducing page load times. Here are some image optimization techniques:

1. **Choose the Right Format**: Use the appropriate image format for the content. JPEG is best for photographs, while PNG is suitable for images with transparency. SVG is ideal for vector graphics.

2. **Resize Images**: Use images with dimensions that match their display size on the website. Avoid using large images and then resizing them with HTML or CSS.

3. **Compress Images**: Compress images to reduce file size while maintaining acceptable quality. Tools like Adobe Photoshop, ImageOptim, or online services like TinyPNG can help.

4. **Lazy Loading**: Implement lazy loading to load images only when they are visible in the user's viewport. This reduces initial page load times.

5. **Use srcset for Responsive Images**: Use the `srcset` attribute to provide multiple image sources at different resolutions. Browsers can then choose the appropriate image based on the user's device.

```
<img
  srcset="image-320w.jpg 320w,
          image-480w.jpg 480w,
          image-800w.jpg 800w"
  sizes="(max-width: 320px) 280px,
         (max-width: 480px) 440px,
         800px"
  src="image-800w.jpg"
  alt="Responsive Image"
/>
```

Video and Audio Optimization

Optimizing video and audio assets is essential for a smooth user experience, especially on mobile devices with limited bandwidth. Here are some optimization techniques:

1. **Choose the Right Format**: Use modern video and audio codecs like H.264 for videos and AAC for audio. These formats offer good quality at lower file sizes.

2. **Compress and Transcode**: Compress video and audio files using tools like HandBrake or FFmpeg. Transcode videos to lower resolutions for different devices.

3. **Streaming**: Implement video and audio streaming for larger media files. This allows users to start watching or listening before the entire file is downloaded.

4. **Poster Images**: Use poster images for videos to display a static image before the video starts loading. This enhances the user experience and provides a visual cue.

```
<video controls poster="video-poster.jpg">
  <source src="video.mp4" type="video/mp4" />
  Your browser does not support the video tag.
</video>
```

5. **Audio Preloading**: For audio files, consider preloading them in the background to reduce playback latency.

```
<audio preload="auto" controls>
  <source src="audio.mp3" type="audio/mpeg" />
  Your browser does not support the audio element.
</audio>
```

Content Delivery Networks (CDNs)

Consider using Content Delivery Networks like Cloudflare, Akamai, or Amazon CloudFront to distribute multimedia assets across multiple servers worldwide. CDNs cache and deliver content from servers closest to the user's location, reducing latency and speeding up content delivery.

Testing and Monitoring

Regularly test your website's performance using tools like Google PageSpeed Insights, GTmetrix, or WebPageTest. Monitor the loading times of multimedia assets and optimize further if necessary. Regular maintenance ensures that your website continues to provide a fast and responsive user experience.

Optimizing multimedia assets is an ongoing process in web design. By following these techniques and staying up to date with best practices, you can ensure that your website loads quickly and efficiently, even when it includes various multimedia elements. This enhances user satisfaction and can positively impact your website's search engine ranking.

Section 13.5: Interactive Media with HTML5 Canvas

HTML5 Canvas is a powerful and versatile feature that allows web developers to create interactive graphics, animations, and games directly within a web page. In this section, we'll explore the capabilities of HTML5 Canvas and how to leverage it to build engaging interactive content.

Introduction to HTML5 Canvas

HTML5 Canvas is an HTML element that provides a blank rectangular area on which you can draw and manipulate graphics using JavaScript. It is resolution-dependent, which means you can create graphics that adapt to various screen sizes and resolutions.

To create a Canvas element, you can use the following HTML:

```
<canvas id="myCanvas" width="800" height="400"></canvas>
```

Drawing on the Canvas

Once you have a Canvas element in your HTML, you can use JavaScript to draw on it. The Canvas API provides a wide range of drawing methods, including lines, shapes, text, and images. Here's an example of drawing a blue rectangle:

```
const canvas = document.getElementById("myCanvas");
const ctx = canvas.getContext("2d");

ctx.fillStyle = "blue";
ctx.fillRect(50, 50, 200, 100);
```

Animation with Canvas

Canvas is commonly used for creating animations. You can create smooth animations by repeatedly redrawing the Canvas with slight variations. To achieve this, you can use the requestAnimationFrame method, which provides a smoother and more efficient way to handle animations than setInterval.

```
function animate() {
  // Clear the canvas
  ctx.clearRect(0, 0, canvas.width, canvas.height);

  // Update and draw your animation here

  // Request the next animation frame
  requestAnimationFrame(animate);
}

// Start the animation
animate();
```

Interactivity

HTML5 Canvas allows you to make your graphics interactive by capturing user input. You can listen for mouse events (e.g., click, move) or touch events (for mobile devices) and respond accordingly. For example, you can create a simple drawing app that lets users draw on the Canvas using their mouse or finger.

```
let isDrawing = false;

canvas.addEventListener("mousedown", () => {
  isDrawing = true;
});

canvas.addEventListener("mousemove", (e) => {
  if (!isDrawing) return;

  ctx.lineWidth = 5;
  ctx.lineCap = "round";
  ctx.strokeStyle = "black";

  ctx.lineTo(e.clientX - canvas.getBoundingClientRect().left, e.clientY -
canvas.getBoundingClientRect().top);
  ctx.stroke();
});

canvas.addEventListener("mouseup", () => {
  isDrawing = false;
});

canvas.addEventListener("mouseout", () => {
  isDrawing = false;
});
```

Libraries and Frameworks

To simplify complex Canvas animations and interactions, you can also consider using libraries and frameworks like Three.js (for 3D graphics), PixiJS (for 2D graphics and games), or Konva.js (for interactive drawings and diagrams).

HTML5 Canvas opens up a world of creative possibilities for web designers and developers. With its ability to create interactive graphics and animations, you can engage and captivate your website's visitors in unique and exciting ways. Whether you're building games, data visualizations, or interactive infographics, HTML5 Canvas is a valuable tool in your web design arsenal.

Chapter 14: Website Navigation and Menus

Section 14.1: Designing Navigation Systems

Navigation is a fundamental aspect of web design that significantly impacts user experience. An effective navigation system ensures that users can find the information they need and move around a website with ease. In this section, we will explore the principles of designing navigation systems and creating user-friendly menus.

Importance of Navigation Design

Navigation design plays a crucial role in shaping the user's journey through a website. A well-designed navigation system can:

1. **Improve Usability**: Intuitive navigation makes it easier for users to access content and complete tasks, reducing frustration and increasing satisfaction.

2. **Enhance User Engagement**: Clear navigation encourages users to explore more pages and spend more time on your site, leading to increased engagement.

3. **Boost Conversions**: Effective navigation can guide users towards important conversion points, such as making a purchase or filling out a contact form.

Types of Navigation

There are several types of navigation commonly used in web design:

- **Top Navigation**: A horizontal menu typically located at the top of the webpage. It often includes primary sections or categories.

- **Sidebar Navigation**: Vertical menus placed on the side of the content area. Sidebar navigation is common in blogs and content-heavy websites.

- **Footer Navigation**: Navigation links placed at the bottom of the page, usually containing secondary or less frequently accessed links.

- **Hamburger Menu**: A compact icon-based menu that expands when clicked or tapped. Commonly used in mobile and responsive designs.

Navigation Best Practices

When designing navigation systems, consider the following best practices:

1. **Keep It Simple**: Avoid overwhelming users with too many menu items. Use concise and clear labels for navigation links.

2. **Prioritize Content**: Place the most important and frequently accessed content in prominent positions, such as the top navigation.

3. **Consistency**: Maintain consistent navigation across all pages of your website. Users should easily recognize and understand the navigation structure.

4. **Responsive Design**: Ensure that navigation menus work well on various devices and screen sizes. Test mobile and tablet views to guarantee usability.

5. **Accessibility**: Follow web accessibility guidelines to make navigation usable for people with disabilities. Provide text alternatives for icons, and ensure keyboard navigation is supported.

6. **Visual Clarity**: Use visual cues like color, hover effects, or highlighting to indicate active links and menu items. Users should always know where they are.

7. **Testing and Iteration**: Regularly test your navigation system with real users and gather feedback. Use analytics to identify any issues and make improvements.

Mega Menus and Dropdowns

For websites with a large amount of content, mega menus and dropdowns can be effective solutions. Mega menus display multiple levels of navigation in a single, visually engaging panel. Dropdown menus, on the other hand, reveal sub-navigation options when a parent menu item is hovered or clicked.

Here's a basic example of an HTML structure for a dropdown menu:

```html
<nav>
  <ul>
    <li><a href="#">Home</a></li>
    <li>
      <a href="#">Products</a>
      <ul>
        <li><a href="#">Product 1</a></li>
        <li><a href="#">Product 2</a></li>
        <!-- Add more product links as needed -->
      </ul>
    </li>
    <li><a href="#">Services</a></li>
    <!-- Add more top-level menu items as needed -->
```

```
    </ul>
</nav>
```

In summary, effective navigation design is essential for creating user-friendly websites. Consider the type of content you have and the needs of your users when deciding on the navigation structure. Keep it simple, consistent, and accessible, and be open to iterative improvements based on user feedback and analytics data.

Section 14.2: Creating Responsive Navigation Bars

Responsive web design is crucial in today's multi-device landscape, where users access websites on various screen sizes, from desktop monitors to smartphones and tablets. In this section, we will explore how to create responsive navigation bars that adapt to different devices and provide an excellent user experience.

The Importance of Responsive Navigation

Responsive navigation bars ensure that your website remains user-friendly and accessible on all devices. Here are some reasons why responsive navigation is essential:

1. **Mobile Optimization**: With the increasing use of mobile devices, responsive navigation ensures that your website is easily navigable on small screens. It prevents users from struggling with tiny, unclickable links.

2. **Improved User Experience**: Responsive navigation contributes to a seamless and enjoyable user experience, reducing bounce rates and improving engagement.

3. **SEO Benefits**: Google and other search engines prioritize mobile-friendly websites in search results. Responsive design, including navigation, can boost your site's search engine ranking.

4. **Consistency**: Maintaining consistent navigation across devices enhances brand identity and user recognition.

Techniques for Responsive Navigation

1. Hamburger Menu

The hamburger menu is a widely used responsive design pattern for mobile navigation. It consists of three horizontal lines that, when clicked or tapped, reveal a hidden menu. Here's an example of HTML and CSS for a basic hamburger menu:

```html
<!-- HTML Structure -->
<div class="menu-toggle">
   <div class="bar"></div>
   <div class="bar"></div>
   <div class="bar"></div>
</div>
```

```
<nav class="mobile-menu">
  <ul>
    <li><a href="#">Home</a></li>
    <li><a href="#">About</a></li>
    <li><a href="#">Services</a></li>
    <!-- Add more menu items as needed -->
  </ul>
</nav>

/* CSS Styles */
.menu-toggle {
  display: none;
  cursor: pointer;
}

.bar {
  width: 30px;
  height: 3px;
  background-color: #333;
  margin: 6px 0;
}

@media (max-width: 768px) {
  .menu-toggle {
    display: block;
  }

  .mobile-menu {
    display: none;
  }

  .menu-open .mobile-menu {
    display: block;
  }
}
```

2. Media Queries

Use CSS media queries to adjust the navigation layout based on screen width. You can switch from a horizontal navigation bar to a vertical one for smaller screens or make other adjustments as needed. Here's an example of a media query for changing navigation styles:

```
/* CSS Styles */
/* Default navigation styles for larger screens */

@media (max-width: 768px) {
  /* Styles for screens with a maximum width of 768px (e.g., tablets and
mobile devices) */
}
```

3. Flexbox and Grid Layout

CSS Flexbox and Grid Layout are powerful tools for creating responsive navigation. They allow you to control the layout and alignment of navigation items easily. For example, you can use Flexbox to create horizontally aligned navigation links and switch to a vertical layout on smaller screens.

Testing and Debugging

After implementing responsive navigation, thoroughly test it on different devices and screen sizes. Ensure that all links are clickable and that the navigation remains user-friendly. Debug any issues that may arise, such as overlapping elements or alignment problems.

In conclusion, responsive navigation is a vital aspect of modern web design. It ensures that users can access your website seamlessly on various devices. Implement techniques like the hamburger menu, media queries, and layout frameworks to create responsive navigation bars that enhance user experience and improve your site's performance on search engines.

Section 14.3: Dropdown Menus and Mega Menus

Dropdown menus are a common navigation pattern used to organize and display a hierarchical list of links or options. In this section, we'll explore how to create dropdown menus and mega menus to enhance the navigation experience on your website.

Dropdown Menus

Dropdown menus are useful when you have a limited number of top-level navigation items that expand to reveal sub-level items when hovered or clicked. Here's how you can create a simple HTML and CSS dropdown menu:

```
<!-- HTML Structure -->
<nav class="dropdown-menu">
  <ul>
    <li><a href="#">Home</a></li>
    <li class="has-submenu">
      <a href="#">Products</a>
      <ul class="submenu">
        <li><a href="#">Product 1</a></li>
        <li><a href="#">Product 2</a></li>
        <!-- Add more sub-menu items as needed -->
      </ul>
    </li>
    <li><a href="#">Services</a></li>
    <!-- Add more top-level menu items as needed -->
  </ul>
</nav>
```

```css
/* CSS Styles */
.dropdown-menu ul {
  list-style: none;
  padding: 0;
  margin: 0;
}

.dropdown-menu li {
  display: inline-block;
  margin-right: 20px;
  position: relative;
}

.has-submenu:hover .submenu {
  display: block;
}

.submenu {
  display: none;
  position: absolute;
  top: 100%;
  left: 0;
  background-color: #fff;
  box-shadow: 0 2px 5px rgba(0, 0, 0, 0.2);
}
```

This code creates a basic dropdown menu that appears when you hover over the "Products" menu item.

Mega Menus

Mega menus are a more extensive version of dropdown menus, typically used for websites with complex navigation structures or e-commerce platforms. They can display a large number of links, images, and additional content in a grid or tabbed layout. Here's an example of an HTML structure for a mega menu:

```html
<!-- HTML Structure -->
<nav class="mega-menu">
  <ul>
    <li><a href="#">Home</a></li>
    <li class="has-mega-menu">
      <a href="#">Products</a>
      <div class="mega-menu-content">
        <div class="row">
          <div class="column">
            <h3>Category 1</h3>
            <ul>
              <li><a href="#">Product 1.1</a></li>
              <li><a href="#">Product 1.2</a></li>
              <!-- Add more product links as needed -->
```

```html
          </ul>
        </div>
        <div class="column">
          <h3>Category 2</h3>
          <ul>
            <li><a href="#">Product 2.1</a></li>
            <li><a href="#">Product 2.2</a></li>
            <!-- Add more product links as needed -->
          </ul>
        </div>
      </div>
    </div>
  </li>
  <li><a href="#">Services</a></li>
  <!-- Add more top-level menu items as needed -->
  </ul>
</nav>
```

```css
/* CSS Styles */
.mega-menu ul {
  list-style: none;
  padding: 0;
  margin: 0;
}

.mega-menu li {
  display: inline-block;
  margin-right: 20px;
  position: relative;
}

.has-mega-menu:hover .mega-menu-content {
  display: block;
}

.mega-menu-content {
  display: none;
  position: absolute;
  top: 100%;
  left: 0;
  background-color: #fff;
  box-shadow: 0 2px 5px rgba(0, 0, 0, 0.2);
  width: 600px;
  padding: 20px;
}

.row {
  display: flex;
  justify-content: space-between;
}
```

```css
.column {
  flex: 1;
  margin-right: 20px;
}
```

This code creates a mega menu that displays product categories and links in a multi-column layout.

Customization and Styling

Dropdown and mega menus can be customized to match your website's design and branding. You can adjust colors, fonts, spacing, and animations to create a visually appealing and user-friendly navigation experience. Additionally, consider making your menus accessible to all users, including those with disabilities, by providing keyboard navigation and ARIA attributes when necessary.

In summary, dropdown menus and mega menus are valuable tools for organizing and presenting your website's content. Depending on your site's complexity and requirements, you can choose between a simple dropdown menu or a more extensive mega menu to improve navigation and user engagement.

Section 14.4: Breadcrumbs and Sitemaps

Breadcrumbs and sitemaps are essential elements of web design that enhance user navigation and provide a clear structure to your website. In this section, we'll explore the benefits of breadcrumbs and sitemaps, how to implement them, and their impact on user experience.

Breadcrumbs

Breadcrumbs are a navigation aid that helps users understand their current location within a website's hierarchy. They are usually displayed horizontally at the top of a webpage and show the path from the homepage to the current page. Here's an example of how breadcrumbs look:

```html
<!-- HTML Structure for Breadcrumbs -->
<div class="breadcrumbs">
  <a href="/">Home</a> >
  <a href="/products">Products</a> >
  <span>Product Name</span>
</div>
```

Breadcrumbs are not only useful for users but also for search engines, as they provide a clear hierarchy of your site's pages. To implement breadcrumbs, you can use HTML and CSS to style them and dynamically generate the links based on the page's location within the site structure.

Sitemaps

A sitemap is a file that provides information about the pages, videos, and other files on your website and how they are related. It helps search engines index your site's content more efficiently, ensuring that your pages are discoverable by users through search results. Sitemaps are typically provided in XML format and submitted to search engines like Google for indexing.

Here's an example of a simple XML sitemap:

```
<!-- XML Sitemap Example -->
<?xml version="1.0" encoding="UTF-8"?>
<urlset xmlns="http://www.sitemaps.org/schemas/sitemap/0.9">
  <url>
    <loc>https://www.example.com/</loc>
    <lastmod>2023-10-01</lastmod>
    <changefreq>weekly</changefreq>
    <priority>1.0</priority>
  </url>
  <url>
    <loc>https://www.example.com/products</loc>
    <lastmod>2023-10-01</lastmod>
    <changefreq>weekly</changefreq>
    <priority>0.8</priority>
  </url>
  <!-- Add more URLs as needed -->
</urlset>
```

You can generate a sitemap manually or use various online tools and plugins for popular content management systems like WordPress. Once generated, you can submit your sitemap to search engines via their respective webmaster tools.

Benefits of Breadcrumbs and Sitemaps

1. **Improved User Experience**: Breadcrumbs provide a clear path for users to navigate back to higher-level pages, making it easier for them to explore your website.

2. **SEO Benefits**: Sitemaps help search engines discover and index your website's content more effectively, potentially improving your site's search engine rankings.

3. **Reduced Bounce Rate**: Users are more likely to stay on your site and explore additional pages when they can easily find related content through breadcrumbs.

4. **Enhanced Accessibility**: Breadcrumbs improve accessibility by providing a visible and structured way for screen readers and keyboard users to understand the site's hierarchy.

5. **Clear Site Structure**: Both breadcrumbs and sitemaps provide a visual representation of your website's structure, helping users and search engines understand how content is organized.

Incorporating breadcrumbs and sitemaps into your web design can significantly enhance user navigation, accessibility, and search engine optimization, contributing to a better overall user experience. Consider implementing these elements as part of your website's design and SEO strategy.

Section 14.5: Accessibility in Navigation Design

Accessibility is a critical aspect of web design that ensures your website can be used by individuals with disabilities. When it comes to navigation design, making your site's menus and navigation elements accessible is essential for providing an inclusive and user-friendly experience. In this section, we'll explore the principles of accessible navigation design and techniques to implement them effectively.

1. Semantic HTML

Use semantic HTML elements for navigation menus and links. Semantically correct elements like <nav>, <ul>, <li>, and <a> convey the structure and purpose of your navigation to assistive technologies. Here's an example:

```
<nav>
  <ul>
    <li><a href="/">Home</a></li>
    <li><a href="/products">Products</a></li>
    <li><a href="/services">Services</a></li>
    <!-- Add more menu items -->
  </ul>
</nav>
```

2. Keyboard Navigation

Ensure that all interactive elements, including navigation menus, can be easily navigated and activated using a keyboard alone. Users who rely on keyboard navigation should be able to access all menu items and submenus without difficulty. Use CSS to highlight the focused element for better visibility.

3. Skip Links

Include skip links at the beginning of your page to allow keyboard users to bypass repetitive navigation menus and jump directly to the main content. These links are typically hidden and become visible when focused. Here's an example:

```
<a href="#main-content" class="skip-link">Skip to main content</a>
```

4. ARIA Roles and Attributes

Use ARIA (Accessible Rich Internet Applications) roles and attributes to enhance the accessibility of complex navigation patterns, such as dropdown menus and accordions.

ARIA can provide additional information to screen readers about the behavior and structure of these elements.

5. Contrast and Color

Ensure that the color contrast between text and background in your navigation menus meets accessibility standards. Low-contrast text can be difficult for users with visual impairments to read. Test your color choices using accessibility evaluation tools.

6. Responsive Design

Make sure your navigation menus are responsive and work well on different devices and screen sizes. On smaller screens, consider using a mobile-friendly menu icon or a collapsible navigation menu to conserve screen space.

7. Testing with Assistive Technologies

Regularly test your website's navigation with assistive technologies such as screen readers and voice recognition software. This helps identify and fix accessibility issues that may arise during navigation.

8. User Testing

Conduct user testing with individuals who have disabilities to gather feedback and make improvements. Real-world feedback from users with disabilities can be invaluable in optimizing your navigation design for accessibility.

By implementing these accessibility principles and techniques in your navigation design, you can ensure that your website is inclusive and usable by a wide range of users. Accessibility not only benefits individuals with disabilities but also improves the overall user experience for everyone.

Chapter 15: Web Forms and User Input

Section 15.1: Building Effective Web Forms

Web forms are a fundamental part of many websites and web applications, allowing users to input data, submit requests, and interact with the site. Creating effective web forms is crucial for a positive user experience. In this section, we will explore the key principles and best practices for building web forms that are user-friendly and functional.

1. Understanding the Purpose

Before designing a web form, it's essential to understand its purpose. What information are you trying to collect from users? Are you creating a contact form, a registration form, or a search form? Clearly define the purpose and the data you need to collect.

2. Form Elements

Web forms consist of various form elements such as text fields, radio buttons, checkboxes, dropdown lists, and buttons. Choose the appropriate form elements that match the type of data you are collecting. Use labels to describe each form element clearly.

3. Organizing and Grouping

Group related form elements together using fieldset and legend elements. For example, if you have a set of radio buttons for gender selection, enclose them within a fieldset and provide a legend like "Gender."

4. Validation and Error Handling

Implement client-side validation to provide immediate feedback to users when they enter invalid data. Common validation includes checking for required fields, email formats, and password strength. Display clear error messages and indicate the specific fields that need correction.

```
<input type="text" id="email" name="email" required pattern="[a-zA-Z0-9._%+-
]+@[a-zA-Z0-9.-]+\.[a-zA-Z-Z]{2,4}">
<span class="error">Please enter a valid email address.</span>
```

5. Accessibility

Ensure that your web forms are accessible to users with disabilities. Use semantic HTML elements and provide appropriate ARIA roles and attributes. Label form elements correctly and use descriptive text for error messages.

6. Mobile-Friendly Design

Design your web forms to be responsive and mobile-friendly. Consider the smaller screen sizes of mobile devices and ensure that form elements are easy to tap and interact with on touch screens.

7. Submission Handling

Define how form submissions will be handled. Will data be sent to a server for processing? Use server-side validation and security measures to prevent data manipulation.

8. User Feedback

After a user submits a form, provide clear feedback. Let users know that their submission was successful or inform them of any errors. You can use a thank-you page or a modal dialog for this purpose.

9. Testing

Thoroughly test your web forms on different browsers and devices to ensure compatibility. Test form validation, error handling, and submission on both desktop and mobile platforms.

10. Continuous Improvement

Gather feedback from users and monitor form analytics to identify areas for improvement. Make iterative changes to your web forms to enhance the user experience continually.

Building effective web forms is a skill that combines usability, accessibility, and functionality. By following these best practices, you can create web forms that engage users and facilitate data collection effectively.

Section 15.2: Input Validation Techniques

Input validation is a crucial aspect of web form development. It ensures that the data submitted by users is accurate, secure, and adheres to predefined criteria. Without proper input validation, web forms may accept incorrect or malicious data, leading to various issues. In this section, we will explore techniques for validating user input in web forms.

1. Client-Side Validation

Client-side validation is performed on the user's device, typically using JavaScript, before the form is submitted to the server. It provides immediate feedback to users, enhancing the user experience. Common client-side validation techniques include:

- **Required Fields:** Ensure that mandatory fields are filled out before submission.
- **Data Format:** Validate data formats such as email addresses, phone numbers, and dates.
- **Length Limits:** Check the length of input data, e.g., maximum characters for a comment field.
- **Numeric Values:** Validate numeric inputs, ensuring they are within a specified range.

Here's an example of client-side validation using JavaScript for a required email field:

```
<input type="email" id="email" name="email" required>
```

2. Server-Side Validation

Server-side validation is essential to validate data after it is submitted to the server. While client-side validation improves user experience, server-side validation is the final line of defense against incorrect or malicious data. It should never be skipped, as client-side validation can be bypassed.

Common server-side validation techniques include:

- **Data Integrity:** Verify that the submitted data is consistent with the expected data type and format.
- **Database Checks:** Ensure that data submitted to a database is valid and does not contain SQL injection or other attacks.
- **Captcha:** Implement captchas to prevent automated submissions by bots.

3. Regular Expressions

Regular expressions (regex) are powerful patterns for matching and validating strings. They are handy for validating email addresses, phone numbers, and other complex formats. Here's an example of using regex in JavaScript to validate an email address:

```
const emailInput = document.getElementById('email');
const emailPattern = /^[a-zA-Z0-9._%+-]+@[a-zA-Z0-9.-]+\.[a-zA-Z]{2,4}$/;

emailInput.addEventListener('input', function () {
  if (!emailPattern.test(this.value)) {
    // Display an error message or provide feedback to the user.
  }
});
```

4. Whitelisting and Blacklisting

Whitelisting and blacklisting are techniques for allowing or denying specific characters or patterns in user input. Whitelisting only allows specified characters or patterns, while blacklisting blocks specific characters or patterns.

For example, you can whitelist input for a username field to allow only alphanumeric characters and underscores:

```
const usernameInput = document.getElementById('username');
const validCharacters = /^[a-zA-Z0-9_]+$/;

usernameInput.addEventListener('input', function () {
  if (!validCharacters.test(this.value)) {
    // Display an error message or provide feedback to the user.
  }
});
```

5. Sanitization

Data sanitization involves cleaning or filtering input data to remove potentially harmful or unwanted content. For example, you can sanitize user-generated content like comments to remove HTML tags and script elements to prevent cross-site scripting (XSS) attacks.

```
const commentInput = document.getElementById('comment');

commentInput.addEventListener('input', function () {
  // Sanitize input to remove HTML tags and scripts.
  const sanitizedInput = stripHtmlTags(this.value);
  this.value = sanitizedInput;
});
```

Implementing input validation techniques, both on the client-side and server-side, is essential for maintaining the security and integrity of web forms. It helps prevent common issues such as data breaches, injection attacks, and user input errors.

Section 15.3: Styling Form Elements

Styling form elements is an essential aspect of web design as it enhances the user experience and makes your web forms visually appealing. In this section, we will explore various techniques for styling form elements using CSS and some considerations for improving form design.

1. CSS Selectors for Form Elements

CSS provides selectors that specifically target form elements, allowing you to style them individually or collectively. Some commonly used selectors for styling form elements include:

- **Type Selectors:** These selectors target elements by their type, such as `input`, `textarea`, or `select`. For example, you can style all input fields with a particular background color:

  ```
  input {
    background-color: #f2f2f2;
  }
  ```

- **Class and ID Selectors:** Assigning classes or IDs to form elements enables you to style them uniquely. For example, you can style a specific input field with an ID of "username":

  ```
  #username {
    border: 1px solid #ccc;
  }
  ```

- **Attribute Selectors:** You can select elements based on their attributes. For instance, you can style all required fields with a red border:

```
input[required] {
  border: 1px solid red;
}
```

2. Form Layout and Structure

Consider the layout and structure of your forms to make them user-friendly. Proper alignment, grouping related fields, and using clear labels can greatly enhance the form's usability. CSS can help you achieve these goals by controlling margins, padding, and positioning.

- **Field Alignment:** Use CSS to align fields, labels, and buttons consistently. For example, you can align labels to the left of their corresponding input fields:

```
label {
  display: inline-block;
  width: 150px; /* Adjust as needed */
  text-align: right;
  margin-right: 10px;
}
```

- **Field Grouping:** Group related fields using fieldsets and legends. CSS can help you style these elements to create visually appealing groupings.

- **Spacing:** Use margins and padding to control the spacing between form elements. Proper spacing makes the form more readable and accessible.

3. Custom Styling

Customizing the appearance of form elements beyond their default styles is a common practice. You can style input fields, checkboxes, radio buttons, and select dropdowns to match your website's design.

- **Input Fields:** Apply styles like borders, background colors, and fonts to input fields to match your design aesthetic.

- **Checkboxes and Radio Buttons:** Customize the appearance of checkboxes and radio buttons using CSS to create unique styles. You can hide the default styles and use custom graphics.

- **Select Dropdowns:** Style select dropdowns to match your site's color scheme and typography. Be cautious when customizing select boxes as they may behave differently on various browsers.

4. Responsiveness

Ensure that your styled form elements are responsive to different screen sizes. Use media queries in CSS to adjust the styling based on the device's width. This ensures that the form remains usable on mobile devices and desktop screens.

5. Feedback and Validation

Consider providing visual feedback to users when they interact with the form elements. Highlighting focused or hovered elements, displaying error messages, and indicating valid input can improve the user experience.

In summary, styling form elements using CSS is essential for creating user-friendly and visually appealing web forms. Consider the layout, structure, and responsiveness of your forms while customizing the appearance of form elements to match your overall design. Effective styling enhances the user experience and encourages users to interact with your forms.

Section 15.4: Handling Form Submissions with JavaScript

Handling form submissions with JavaScript is a crucial part of web development, especially when you need to validate user input, process data, or interact with a server. In this section, we will explore how to work with form submissions using JavaScript, from capturing user input to handling validation and submission events.

1. Form Elements and JavaScript

To work with form submissions, you need to access form elements using JavaScript. You can do this by targeting elements based on their id, name, or by using other selection methods.

```html
<form id="myForm">
  <input type="text" name="username" id="username">
  <input type="email" name="email" id="email">
  <button type="submit">Submit</button>
</form>

<script>
  const form = document.getElementById("myForm");
  const usernameInput = document.getElementById("username");
  const emailInput = document.getElementById("email");

  form.addEventListener("submit", function(event) {
    event.preventDefault(); // Prevent the default form submission
    // Your submission logic here
  });
</script>
```

In the above example, we access the form and input elements using their id attributes and attach an event listener to the form's submit event.

2. Form Validation

Validating user input before submission is essential to ensure data integrity and security. JavaScript can help you implement various validation checks, such as checking for required fields, verifying email formats, or ensuring password strength.

```javascript
form.addEventListener("submit", function(event) {
  event.preventDefault();

  const username = usernameInput.value;
  const email = emailInput.value;

  if (username === "" || email === "") {
    alert("Please fill in all required fields.");
    return;
  }

  // Additional validation logic for email format, password strength, etc.

  // If all validation checks pass, you can proceed with form submission.
});
```

3. Asynchronous Form Submission

In many cases, you'll need to send data to a server for processing without reloading the entire page. This can be achieved using AJAX (Asynchronous JavaScript and XML) or the modern Fetch API.

```javascript
form.addEventListener("submit", function(event) {
  event.preventDefault();

  const formData = new FormData(form);

  fetch("submit.php", {
    method: "POST",
    body: formData
  })
  .then(response => response.json())
  .then(data => {
    // Handle the server's response
  })
  .catch(error => {
    console.error("Error:", error);
  });
});
```

In the example above, we use the Fetch API to send form data to a server-side script (submit.php) asynchronously. You can replace "submit.php" with the appropriate URL for your backend.

4. Feedback to Users

Providing feedback to users after form submission is important. You can display success messages or error messages on the page or redirect users to a different page.

```javascript
form.addEventListener("submit", function(event) {
  event.preventDefault();

  // Validation checks here

  if (validationPassed) {
    // Submit the form asynchronously
    fetch("submit.php", {
      method: "POST",
      body: formData
    })
    .then(response => response.json())
    .then(data => {
      // Display a success message to the user
      alert("Form submitted successfully!");
      // You can also redirect the user to a thank you page
      window.location.href = "thank-you.html";
    })
    .catch(error => {
      console.error("Error:", error);
    });
  } else {
    // Display an error message to the user
    alert("Form submission failed. Please check your inputs.");
  }
});
```

In this example, if the form submission is successful, we display an alert with a success message and optionally redirect the user to a thank you page. If there are validation errors or server-side issues, an error message is displayed to the user.

5. Security Considerations

When handling form submissions with JavaScript, be mindful of security. Always sanitize and validate user inputs on the server-side to prevent security vulnerabilities like SQL injection or Cross-Site Scripting (XSS).

In summary, handling form submissions with JavaScript involves accessing form elements, performing client-side validation, and potentially sending data to a server asynchronously. Providing feedback to users and ensuring security are essential aspects of form submission handling in web development.

Section 15.5: Captchas and Security Measures

In modern web development, security is paramount, especially when dealing with user inputs and forms. Captchas are an essential security measure used to distinguish between human users and automated bots. In this section, we will explore what captchas are, how to implement them, and other security measures to protect your web forms.

1. What Are Captchas?

A CAPTCHA (Completely Automated Public Turing test to tell Computers and Humans Apart) is a challenge-response test designed to determine whether the user is a human or a bot. Captchas typically involve tasks that are easy for humans to solve but challenging for automated scripts.

Common captcha types include:

- **Image-based captchas:** Users must identify and select specific objects or characters within an image.
- **Text-based captchas:** Users must enter text displayed in an image or distorted text that's difficult for bots to read.
- **Checkbox captchas:** Users must check a box to confirm they are not a robot.
- **ReCAPTCHA:** A more advanced version that uses machine learning to determine user authenticity.

2. Implementing Captchas

To implement a captcha in your web form, you can use third-party services like Google's reCAPTCHA, which provides a JavaScript API for integration. Here's a simplified example of how to add reCAPTCHA to your form:

```
<!-- Include reCAPTCHA script -->
<script src="https://www.google.com/recaptcha/api.js" async defer></script>

<form>
  <!-- Your form fields here -->

  <!-- reCAPTCHA widget -->
  <div class="g-recaptcha" data-sitekey="YOUR_SITE_KEY"></div>

  <button type="submit">Submit</button>
</form>
```

In the example above, replace "YOUR_SITE_KEY" with your reCAPTCHA site key obtained from the reCAPTCHA website. When the user submits the form, the reCAPTCHA widget will validate whether the user is human.

3. Other Security Measures

Besides captchas, there are additional security measures you should consider when working with web forms:

- **Input Validation:** Implement strong input validation on the server-side to prevent malicious inputs. Check for SQL injection, XSS attacks, and other vulnerabilities.

- **HTTPS:** Use HTTPS to encrypt data transmission between the client and server, ensuring that sensitive information is secure during submission.

- **Rate Limiting:** Implement rate limiting to prevent brute force attacks on forms.

- **Input Sanitization:** Sanitize and filter user inputs to remove potentially harmful content.

- **Authentication and Authorization:** Implement user authentication and authorization mechanisms to control access to sensitive forms and data.

- **Session Management:** Use secure session management practices to prevent session hijacking.

- **Data Validation:** Validate and sanitize data before processing it on the server-side. Ensure data consistency and integrity.

4. The Importance of Security

Security is not a one-time consideration; it should be an ongoing process in web development. Implementing captchas and other security measures helps protect your forms and user data from malicious actors and automated scripts. Regularly update and audit your security measures to stay ahead of potential threats and vulnerabilities.

In summary, captchas are essential for verifying user authenticity and protecting web forms from automated bots. Implementing reCAPTCHA and combining it with other security measures is crucial to ensure the security of your web applications and user data.

Chapter 16: Search Engine Optimization (SEO)

Section 16.1: SEO Basics and Importance

Search Engine Optimization, commonly referred to as SEO, is a fundamental aspect of web design and digital marketing. It encompasses various strategies and techniques aimed at improving a website's visibility on search engines like Google, Bing, and Yahoo. In this section, we'll delve into the basics of SEO and why it's crucial for web designers and developers to understand and implement.

What Is SEO?

SEO is the practice of optimizing a website so that it ranks higher in search engine results pages (SERPs) for relevant keywords and phrases. The primary goal of SEO is to increase organic (non-paid) traffic to a website by improving its search engine ranking. When a website appears higher in search results, it is more likely to receive clicks and visits from users.

The Importance of SEO

1. **Enhanced Visibility:** Websites that appear on the first page of search results are more likely to be noticed by users. Improved visibility can lead to more traffic and potential customers.

2. **Credibility and Trust:** Websites ranking high in search results are often perceived as more credible and trustworthy by users. A good SEO strategy can help build a positive online reputation.

3. **Cost-Effective Marketing:** Compared to paid advertising, SEO is a cost-effective way to attract organic traffic. It can provide long-term results without the need for continuous ad spending.

4. **Targeted Traffic:** SEO allows you to target specific keywords and phrases relevant to your business or content. This means that the traffic you receive is more likely to be interested in what you offer.

5. **Competitive Advantage:** Many of your competitors are likely investing in SEO. By having an effective SEO strategy, you can gain a competitive edge in your industry.

Key SEO Elements

To achieve effective SEO, web designers and developers need to consider several key elements:

- **On-Page Optimization:** This involves optimizing individual web pages by focusing on factors such as keyword optimization, meta tags, headers, and content quality.

- **Technical SEO:** Technical aspects of a website, including site speed, mobile-friendliness, and crawlability, can significantly impact search rankings.

- **Link Building:** Building high-quality backlinks from reputable websites can boost a site's authority and ranking.

- **Content Strategy:** Creating high-quality, relevant, and engaging content is a core component of SEO. Content should be tailored to target keywords and provide value to users.

- **User Experience (UX):** A positive user experience, including fast page loading times and easy navigation, is crucial for both SEO and user satisfaction.

SEO and Web Design

Web designers play a vital role in SEO by creating websites that are not only visually appealing but also optimized for search engines. This includes ensuring that websites are mobile-responsive, have clean and crawlable code, and provide a seamless user experience. Collaboration between web designers and SEO specialists is essential to achieve the best results.

In conclusion, SEO is a critical aspect of web design and digital marketing. Understanding its basics and importance is essential for web designers and developers who aim to create websites that perform well in search engine rankings. By incorporating SEO best practices into web design, you can increase a website's visibility, credibility, and overall success on the web.

Section 16.2: On-Page SEO Techniques

On-page SEO refers to the optimization efforts that are applied directly to the web pages of a website to improve their search engine rankings. These techniques focus on factors that you have control over within your content and HTML code. In this section, we'll explore various on-page SEO techniques that web designers and developers can implement to enhance a website's visibility and ranking in search results.

1. Keyword Research

Keyword research is the foundation of on-page SEO. It involves identifying the keywords and phrases that your target audience is likely to use when searching for your content or products. Tools like Google Keyword Planner, Ahrefs, and SEMrush can help you discover relevant keywords with sufficient search volume. Once you've identified your target keywords, incorporate them naturally into your content.

Example:
```
If you're writing a blog post about "healthy smoothie recipes," ensure that
the target keyword "healthy smoothie recipes" is used in the title, headings,
and throughout the content.
```

2. High-Quality Content

Content is king in the world of SEO. Google and other search engines prioritize websites that provide valuable, informative, and engaging content. Create content that addresses the needs and interests of your target audience. Longer, comprehensive articles tend to perform well in search rankings.

3. Optimized Titles and Headings

The title of your web page is a crucial on-page SEO element. It should be concise, descriptive, and contain the target keyword. Use heading tags (H1, H2, H3, etc.) to structure your content logically. The H1 tag should contain the main topic or focus keyword of the page.

Example:
```html
<h1>Healthy Smoothie Recipes for a Nutrient-Packed Breakfast</h1>
```

4. Meta Tags

Meta tags provide information about a web page to search engines. The two most important meta tags are the meta title and meta description. These should be unique for each page and include the target keyword.

Example:
```html
<title>Healthy Smoothie Recipes - Nutrient-Packed Breakfast Ideas</title>
<meta name="description" content="Explore our collection of healthy smoothie recipes that are perfect for a nutritious breakfast. Get inspired with a variety of flavors and ingredients.">
```

5. Image Optimization

Optimize images by reducing their file size without compromising quality. Use descriptive filenames and include alt text for images to improve accessibility and provide context to search engines.

Example:
```html
<img src="smoothie.jpg" alt="Blueberry and Banana Smoothie" />
```

6. Internal Linking

Internal links help search engines understand the structure and hierarchy of your website. Link to relevant internal pages within your content using descriptive anchor text.

Example:
```html
<a href="/recipes/strawberry-smoothie">Check out our delicious strawberry smoothie recipe</a>
```

7. Mobile-Friendly Design

Ensure that your website is responsive and mobile-friendly. Google considers mobile-friendliness as a ranking factor, and a poor mobile experience can negatively impact your rankings.

8. Page Speed

Page speed is crucial for both user experience and SEO. Compress images, minimize code, and leverage browser caching to improve loading times.

9. User-Friendly URLs

Create user-friendly URLs that are easy to read and contain relevant keywords. Avoid lengthy and cryptic URLs.

Example:
```html
https://www.example.com/healthy-smoothie-recipes
```

10. Schema Markup

Schema markup provides additional context to search engines about your content. Implement schema markup for reviews, recipes, events, and other structured data to enhance your search listings.

Example:
```html
<script type="application/ld+json">
{
  "@context": "http://schema.org",
  "@type": "Recipe",
  "name": "Healthy Green Smoothie",
  "author": "John Doe",
  "datePublished": "2023-04-15",
  "description": "A nutritious green smoothie recipe with spinach, kale, and avocado.",
  "image": "smoothie.jpg",
  "recipeIngredient": [
    "1 cup spinach",
    "1/2 cup kale",
    "1/2 avocado",
    "1 cup almond milk",
    "1 tablespoon honey"
  ],
  "recipeInstructions": "..."
}
</script>
```

Implementing these on-page SEO techniques can significantly improve your website's search engine rankings. Remember that SEO is an ongoing process, and regularly updating and optimizing your content is essential for maintaining and improving your rankings over time.

Section 16.3: SEO Tools and Analytics

Search engine optimization (SEO) is an evolving field, and web designers and developers need to stay informed about how their websites are performing in search results. This requires the use of various SEO tools and analytics platforms to monitor, analyze, and improve your website's SEO strategy. In this section, we'll explore some essential SEO tools and analytics platforms that can help you achieve better search engine rankings and user engagement.

1. Google Analytics

Google Analytics is one of the most popular and powerful web analytics tools available. It provides valuable insights into website traffic, user behavior, and conversions. By integrating Google Analytics with your website, you can track important metrics such as the number of visitors, pageviews, bounce rate, and more. This data helps you make informed decisions about your content and SEO strategy.

2. Google Search Console

Google Search Console is a free tool provided by Google that allows you to monitor and manage how your website appears in Google search results. It provides information about indexing status, crawl errors, and keyword performance. You can submit sitemaps, request the removal of outdated content, and identify SEO issues that need attention.

3. Ahrefs

Ahrefs is a comprehensive SEO toolset that includes features for keyword research, backlink analysis, competitor analysis, and more. It helps you identify the keywords that drive traffic to your website, discover your competitors' top-performing pages, and track the growth of your backlink profile.

4. SEMrush

SEMrush is another popular SEO tool that offers a wide range of features, including keyword research, competitive analysis, and site audit. It helps you identify valuable keywords, track your keyword rankings, and analyze your competitors' strategies. SEMrush also provides insights into paid advertising and social media performance.

5. Moz Pro

Moz Pro offers a suite of SEO tools designed to improve your website's search engine rankings. It provides features for keyword research, rank tracking, site audits, and link analysis. Moz's Domain Authority metric is widely used to assess the authority of websites and domains.

6. Screaming Frog SEO Spider

Screaming Frog SEO Spider is a website crawler that helps you identify technical SEO issues. It can crawl your website to find broken links, duplicate content, and other on-page SEO problems. This tool is particularly useful for larger websites with many pages.

7. Yoast SEO (WordPress Plugin)

If your website is built on WordPress, the Yoast SEO plugin is a must-have. It helps you optimize your content for SEO by providing recommendations for improving readability, keyword usage, and meta tags. It also generates XML sitemaps and handles technical SEO aspects.

8. Google PageSpeed Insights

Page speed is a critical factor for SEO and user experience. Google PageSpeed Insights analyzes your website's performance and provides suggestions for improving page load times. It also assesses your website's mobile-friendliness.

9. Bing Webmaster Tools

While Google dominates the search engine market, it's essential not to overlook Bing. Bing Webmaster Tools offers insights into how your website performs on Bing search, including keyword rankings, crawl errors, and sitemap submission.

10. Rank Math (WordPress Plugin)

Similar to Yoast SEO, Rank Math is a popular SEO plugin for WordPress. It offers features like on-page SEO analysis, XML sitemaps, schema markup, and social media integration. It's a user-friendly alternative for WordPress users looking to enhance their SEO efforts.

Using these SEO tools and analytics platforms, you can gain a deeper understanding of your website's performance, identify areas for improvement, and implement effective SEO strategies to increase your visibility in search engine results pages (SERPs). Regularly monitoring and optimizing your website's SEO is essential for maintaining and improving your online presence.

Section 16.4: Content Strategy for SEO

A successful SEO strategy is not only about optimizing your website's technical aspects but also about creating high-quality, relevant, and valuable content that resonates with your target audience. In this section, we'll delve into the importance of content strategy for SEO and explore some key principles to help you craft content that ranks well in search engines.

1. Keyword Research

Keyword research is the foundation of any effective content strategy for SEO. It involves identifying the keywords and phrases that your target audience is searching for. Tools like

Google Keyword Planner, Ahrefs, and SEMrush can help you discover relevant keywords with high search volume and reasonable competition.

Once you've identified your target keywords, integrate them naturally into your content. Focus on creating content that answers users' questions or addresses their needs while incorporating these keywords strategically. Avoid keyword stuffing, which can harm your rankings and user experience.

2. High-Quality and Unique Content

Search engines reward websites that provide high-quality and unique content. When crafting articles, blog posts, or other forms of content, aim for originality and depth. Avoid duplicating content from other sources, as this can result in penalties from search engines.

Your content should provide value, insights, or solutions to the problems your audience faces. Make it informative, engaging, and easy to read. Well-structured content with headings, bullet points, and concise paragraphs is more user-friendly and search engine-friendly.

3. Content Length and Depth

Long-form content tends to perform well in search results. While there's no fixed word count that guarantees success, longer articles (usually 1,500 words or more) often have the space to explore topics comprehensively. This allows you to cover subtopics and related questions, which can improve your content's relevance.

However, always prioritize quality over quantity. Don't pad your content with filler to meet a specific word count. Ensure that every part of your content is valuable and directly contributes to the topic.

4. Mobile-Friendly Content

With the increasing use of mobile devices, having mobile-friendly content is crucial for SEO. Ensure that your website and content are responsive and adapt well to various screen sizes. Google considers mobile-friendliness as a ranking factor, and a poor mobile experience can negatively impact your SEO.

5. User Intent

Understanding user intent is essential for crafting content that matches what users are looking for. Users may have informational, navigational, or transactional intent when performing searches. Tailor your content to align with these intents.

For informational queries, provide in-depth guides, how-to articles, or informative blog posts. For navigational queries, ensure that your content helps users find what they're looking for on your website. For transactional queries, create content that encourages conversions, such as product descriptions, reviews, or pricing information.

6. Regularly Updated Content

Freshness matters in SEO. Regularly update your existing content to keep it relevant and accurate. Outdated information can harm your credibility and rankings. Additionally, Google often rewards websites that consistently publish new, relevant content.

7. Internal and External Links

Incorporate internal links to other relevant pages on your website to help users navigate and discover more of your content. External links to authoritative sources can enhance your content's credibility. When linking, use descriptive anchor text that provides context.

8. Use Schema Markup

Schema markup, also known as structured data, helps search engines understand the content of your pages. It can enhance your search results with rich snippets, such as star ratings for product reviews or event details. Implementing schema markup can make your content more attractive to users and improve click-through rates.

9. Monitoring and Analytics

Regularly monitor the performance of your content using analytics tools like Google Analytics and Google Search Console. Track key metrics such as organic traffic, click-through rates, bounce rates, and keyword rankings. Use these insights to refine your content strategy over time.

10. Content Promotion

Creating great content is only half the battle; promoting it is equally important. Share your content on social media, email newsletters, and relevant online communities. Building backlinks from reputable websites can also boost your content's authority and SEO.

In conclusion, a well-crafted content strategy is a fundamental component of a successful SEO strategy. By conducting thorough keyword research, creating high-quality content, optimizing for mobile, aligning with user intent, and continuously improving your content, you can enhance your website's visibility in search engine results and provide value to your audience.

Section 16.5: Mobile SEO and Voice Search Optimization

As the digital landscape continues to evolve, optimizing your web content for mobile devices and voice search is becoming increasingly important. In this section, we'll explore the significance of mobile SEO and voice search optimization and provide strategies to ensure your website performs well in these contexts.

1. Mobile SEO

Responsive Design:

Mobile-friendliness is a critical ranking factor in search engines. Ensure that your website employs a responsive design, which adapts seamlessly to various screen sizes and orientations. Responsive websites provide a better user experience on mobile devices, which can positively impact your SEO.

Page Speed:

Mobile users expect fast-loading web pages. Google uses page speed as a ranking factor for mobile searches. Optimize your website's performance by minimizing image sizes, leveraging browser caching, and reducing unnecessary code and scripts. Google's PageSpeed Insights tool can help identify areas for improvement.

Mobile-First Indexing:

Google has adopted a mobile-first indexing approach, which means it primarily uses the mobile version of a website for ranking and indexing. Ensure that both your desktop and mobile versions have consistent content and metadata to avoid SEO discrepancies.

Structured Data:

Implement structured data markup, such as Schema.org, to provide additional context to search engines about your content. This can lead to rich snippets in search results, which can improve click-through rates on mobile devices.

Local SEO:

Mobile users often perform "near me" searches to find local businesses. Optimize your website for local SEO by creating a Google My Business profile, obtaining customer reviews, and ensuring your contact information is accurate and consistent across the web.

2. Voice Search Optimization

Natural Language Queries:

Voice search queries tend to be more conversational and natural in tone. Optimize your content by including long-tail keywords and answering questions concisely. Use tools like AnswerThePublic to identify common questions related to your industry.

Featured Snippets:

Voice assistants often read answers from featured snippets in search results. Structure your content to provide clear, concise answers to common queries. Formatting content in bullet points or tables can increase the likelihood of being featured.

Voice searches are frequently used for local queries. Ensure that your business is optimized for voice searches by having accurate business information, including address, phone number, and business hours, readily available on your website.

Mobile Compatibility:

Voice search is predominantly performed on mobile devices. Therefore, the same mobile SEO best practices apply. Focus on providing a fast and mobile-friendly experience for users conducting voice searches.

Conversational Content:

Consider creating content that mimics a conversation with users. This can be in the form of FAQs, chatbots, or interactive guides. Such content aligns well with voice search queries.

Regular Updates:

Voice search technology continues to evolve. Stay updated with voice search trends and adapt your content accordingly. Voice recognition technology is becoming more sophisticated, allowing for better comprehension of natural language.

In conclusion, mobile SEO and voice search optimization are integral components of modern SEO strategies. Ensuring that your website is mobile-friendly, loads quickly, and provides valuable content for voice search queries can enhance your website's visibility and reach in today's digital landscape. By staying attuned to the changing habits of users and search engine algorithms, you can maintain a competitive edge in the world of SEO.

Chapter 17: Web Hosting and Domain Management

Section 17.1: Choosing a Web Hosting Provider

Selecting the right web hosting provider is a crucial decision for your website's success. Your choice will impact your website's performance, reliability, and overall user experience. In this section, we will discuss the key factors to consider when choosing a web hosting provider.

1. Types of Web Hosting

There are various types of web hosting, each catering to different needs:

- **Shared Hosting:** Inexpensive but shares server resources with other websites.
- **VPS (Virtual Private Server) Hosting:** Provides a dedicated portion of a server, offering more control and performance.
- **Dedicated Hosting:** You have an entire server to yourself, ideal for high-traffic websites.

- **Cloud Hosting:** Scalable hosting that utilizes a network of virtual servers.
- **Managed WordPress Hosting:** Optimized for WordPress sites, offering automatic updates and security.

Consider your website's requirements and budget when choosing the hosting type.

2. Uptime and Reliability

Uptime is crucial for your website's accessibility. Look for a hosting provider that guarantees a high uptime percentage, preferably 99.9% or higher. Read user reviews and check if the provider has a history of frequent downtimes.

3. Server Location

The server's physical location can affect your website's speed. Choose a hosting provider with data centers located close to your target audience. This reduces latency and improves loading times.

4. Scalability

Consider your website's growth potential. A good hosting provider should allow you to easily upgrade your hosting plan as your site expands. Scalability ensures your website can handle increased traffic without performance issues.

5. Security Features

Website security is paramount. Check if the hosting provider offers features like SSL certificates, DDoS protection, regular backups, and a Web Application Firewall (WAF). These features help protect your website from threats.

6. Customer Support

Responsive customer support is vital, especially in case of technical issues. Look for hosting providers offering 24/7 customer support through various channels like live chat, email, and phone. Test their support responsiveness before making a decision.

7. Pricing and Renewal Costs

Pay attention to pricing structures. Some providers offer low initial prices but significantly increase renewal costs. Understand the long-term pricing to avoid surprises.

8. Control Panel

A user-friendly control panel (e.g., cPanel or Plesk) makes it easier to manage your website. Ensure your hosting provider offers a control panel that suits your needs.

9. Add-Ons and Extras

Some providers offer additional services like domain registration, website builders, and email hosting. Consider these extras if they align with your requirements.

Read reviews and seek recommendations from peers or online communities. User experiences can provide valuable insights into a hosting provider's performance and reliability.

11. Money-Back Guarantee

Check if the hosting provider offers a money-back guarantee. This allows you to try their services risk-free and ensures you can get a refund if you're dissatisfied.

In conclusion, choosing a web hosting provider requires careful consideration of your website's needs, budget, and performance expectations. Conduct thorough research, read reviews, and consider recommendations to make an informed decision. Remember that a reliable hosting provider is the foundation of a successful online presence.

Section 17.2: Domain Registration and DNS Configuration

Registering a domain name is a critical step in establishing your online presence. Your domain name is your website's address on the internet, making it easy for users to find you. In this section, we will discuss domain registration and Domain Name System (DNS) configuration.

1. Domain Registration

To register a domain name, follow these steps:

- **Choose a Domain Name:** Select a unique and relevant domain name that represents your website or business. Keep it concise and memorable.

- **Check Domain Availability:** Use domain registrar websites or tools to check if your desired domain name is available. If it's already registered, you may need to choose an alternative name.

- **Select a Domain Registrar:** Choose a reputable domain registrar to purchase your domain name. Popular registrars include GoDaddy, Namecheap, Google Domains, and more. Compare prices and features to make an informed decision.

- **Complete Registration:** Provide your contact information and payment details to complete the registration process. Ensure your contact information is accurate to receive important notifications and renewal reminders.

- **Domain Privacy Protection:** Consider adding domain privacy protection (WHOIS privacy) to hide your personal information from the public WHOIS database. This helps protect your privacy and reduce spam.

Once you've registered a domain name, you need to configure DNS settings to point your domain to the correct web server. Here's how:

- **DNS Records:** DNS records are used to map domain names to IP addresses. Common DNS records include A records (IPv4 address), AAAA records (IPv6 address), CNAME records (alias), MX records (mail servers), and TXT records (text information).

- **Name Servers:** Name servers are responsible for resolving domain names to IP addresses. Your domain registrar will provide default name servers, but you can also use custom name servers if you're hosting your website on a specific server.

- **Propagation Time:** After making DNS changes, DNS propagation occurs, which may take some time. During this period, DNS changes are propagated across the internet's DNS servers. It usually takes a few hours to 48 hours for DNS changes to fully propagate.

- **Testing:** Use DNS lookup tools or online DNS checkers to verify that your DNS settings are correctly configured. Ensure that your domain name resolves to the correct IP address.

- **Subdomains:** You can configure subdomains (e.g., blog.yourdomain.com) by adding appropriate DNS records and configuring your web server to handle subdomain requests.

- **Email Configuration:** Configure MX records to handle email services associated with your domain. Ensure that email delivery works correctly.

- **SSL Certificates:** If you're using SSL/TLS for secure connections (HTTPS), you may need to configure SSL certificates and update your DNS settings accordingly.

3. DNS Management

Most domain registrars provide web-based DNS management tools that allow you to edit DNS records and name server settings. It's essential to keep your DNS records up to date, especially if you change web hosting providers or servers.

In conclusion, domain registration and DNS configuration are fundamental aspects of web hosting and domain management. Choose a reliable domain registrar, configure your DNS settings correctly, and regularly monitor and update your DNS records as needed. A well-configured domain and DNS setup ensure that users can access your website and services reliably.

Section 17.3: Uploading Web Files and Databases

Once you've registered a domain name, configured your DNS settings, and set up your web hosting environment, the next step in building a website is uploading your web files and databases to the hosting server. This process is crucial for making your website accessible to users worldwide. In this section, we will explore the steps and considerations for uploading web files and databases.

1. Web File Upload

Uploading web files typically involves transferring your website's HTML, CSS, JavaScript, images, and other assets to the web server. Here's how you can do it:

- **FTP (File Transfer Protocol):** One of the most common methods is using FTP software like FileZilla to connect to your web server. You'll need the FTP server credentials provided by your hosting provider. Once connected, you can drag and drop files to upload them.

- **Web Hosting Control Panels:** Some hosting providers offer web-based control panels like cPanel or Plesk, which include file managers for uploading files. You can log in to your hosting control panel and use the file manager to upload files directly.

- **Version Control Systems:** If you're using version control systems like Git, you can clone your repository to the server. This is particularly useful for web development teams collaborating on a project.

2. Database Upload

If your website relies on databases (e.g., MySQL, PostgreSQL, MongoDB), you'll need to upload your database content to the server as well. Here's how to do it:

- **Database Dump:** Create a database dump or backup of your local database. This typically generates a SQL file containing the database schema and data.

- **Database Management Tools:** Access your hosting control panel or use command-line tools to import the database dump into the server's database system. This step may require creating a new database on the server if you haven't already done so.

- **Configuration Updates:** Ensure that your website's configuration files (e.g., config.php) are updated to use the correct database credentials for the server.

3. Testing

After uploading web files and databases, it's essential to test your website thoroughly. Here are some key areas to check:

- **Website Functionality:** Test all website features and functionality to ensure they work correctly on the live server. This includes links, forms, interactive elements, and user authentication.

- **Database Connectivity:** Verify that your website can connect to and interact with the server's database without errors. Test data retrieval, insertion, and updates.

- **Performance Testing:** Assess the website's performance, including page load times and responsiveness. Optimize your website for speed if necessary.

- **Cross-Browser Compatibility:** Test your website on various web browsers to ensure it displays consistently and functions properly across different platforms.

- **Mobile Responsiveness:** Confirm that your website is mobile-friendly and responsive, adapting to different screen sizes and devices.

4. Backup and Maintenance

Regularly backup your website files and databases on the server. Many hosting providers offer automated backup solutions. This precaution ensures that you can quickly restore your website in case of data loss or unexpected issues.

In conclusion, uploading web files and databases is a critical step in making your website accessible to users. Ensure that you follow secure and reliable methods for file and database transfer. Thoroughly test your website on the live server to catch and resolve any issues. Regular backups and maintenance help keep your website running smoothly.

Section 17.4: SSL Certificates and Security

SSL (Secure Sockets Layer) certificates play a crucial role in securing your website and ensuring the privacy of user data. In this section, we will delve into SSL certificates, their significance, and how to implement them on your web hosting server.

1. What is an SSL Certificate?

An SSL certificate is a digital certificate that encrypts data transmitted between a user's browser and your web server. It ensures that the information exchanged, such as login credentials, payment details, or personal data, remains confidential and secure. When an SSL certificate is installed, your website URL changes from "http://" to "https://" (where the 's' stands for secure).

2. Types of SSL Certificates

There are several types of SSL certificates available, including:

- **Domain Validated (DV) Certificates:** These certificates are the most basic and typically used for personal websites or blogs. They validate domain ownership but do not verify the organization's identity.

- **Organization Validated (OV) Certificates:** OV certificates validate both domain ownership and the organization's details, providing a higher level of trust.

- **Extended Validation (EV) Certificates:** EV certificates offer the highest level of trust and security. They undergo a rigorous validation process to confirm the organization's identity, resulting in a green address bar and the organization's name displayed in the browser.

- **Wildcard Certificates:** Wildcard certificates secure the main domain and all its subdomains. For example, a wildcard certificate for "example.com" would also cover "sub.example.com."

- **Multi-Domain (SAN) Certificates:** SAN certificates allow you to secure multiple domains or subdomains within a single certificate.

3. Obtaining an SSL Certificate

To obtain an SSL certificate, follow these general steps:

- **Choose a Certificate Authority (CA):** Select a trusted CA to purchase your SSL certificate. Popular CAs include DigiCert, Comodo, and Let's Encrypt (which offers free certificates).

- **Generate a Certificate Signing Request (CSR):** This is a file generated on your web server that contains your domain and public key information. You will provide this CSR to the CA during the certificate purchase process.

- **Verify Domain Ownership:** Depending on the certificate type, you may need to complete domain ownership verification through email, DNS records, or other methods.

- **Purchase and Install:** Buy the SSL certificate from the CA and follow their instructions for installation. Many hosting providers offer integration with CAs, simplifying the process.

4. Benefits of SSL Certificates

Implementing SSL certificates on your website offers numerous advantages:

- **Data Security:** SSL encrypts data transmitted between the user and the server, protecting it from interception by malicious actors.

- **Trust and Credibility:** Websites with SSL certificates display a padlock icon and "https://" in the address bar, signaling trust to visitors.

- **SEO Benefits:** Search engines like Google consider SSL as a ranking factor, potentially improving your website's search engine ranking.

- **PCI Compliance:** If you handle online payments, SSL is essential for Payment Card Industry Data Security Standard (PCI DSS) compliance.

5. Maintenance and Renewal

SSL certificates have a validity period, typically ranging from one to two years. It's crucial to keep track of the certificate's expiration date and renew it in advance to avoid disruptions in website security. Many CAs offer automatic renewal options for convenience.

In conclusion, SSL certificates are a fundamental aspect of website security and user trust. They encrypt data, enhance your website's credibility, and offer various types to suit different needs. Regular maintenance, including timely renewal, ensures that your website remains secure and user-friendly.

Section 17.5: Performance Optimization on the Server Side

Optimizing server performance is a crucial aspect of web hosting and can significantly impact your website's speed, reliability, and user experience. In this section, we will explore various techniques and best practices for optimizing server-side performance.

1. Choose the Right Hosting Plan

Selecting the appropriate hosting plan is the first step in optimizing server performance. There are several types of hosting, including shared, virtual private server (VPS), dedicated, and cloud hosting. The choice depends on your website's traffic, resource requirements, and budget. For high-performance websites, VPS or dedicated hosting is often recommended to ensure dedicated resources and better control over server settings.

2. Server Hardware and Resources

If you have control over your server's hardware, consider the following:

- **CPU and RAM:** Ensure your server has sufficient CPU and RAM resources to handle your website's demands. Upgrading these components can lead to improved performance.

- **Solid-State Drives (SSDs):** SSDs are faster than traditional hard disk drives (HDDs) and can significantly reduce data retrieval times. Hosting your website on SSD-based servers can boost performance.

- **Server Location:** Choose a server location that is geographically closer to your target audience to reduce latency and improve loading times.

3. Content Delivery Networks (CDNs)

Implementing a Content Delivery Network (CDN) can dramatically enhance your website's performance. CDNs distribute your website's static assets (e.g., images, CSS, JavaScript) to servers worldwide, allowing users to download content from a server geographically closer to them. This reduces latency and speeds up page loading. Popular CDNs include Cloudflare, Akamai, and Amazon CloudFront.

4. Web Server Software

Selecting the right web server software is critical. Popular choices include Apache, Nginx, and LiteSpeed. Nginx, known for its speed and efficiency in handling concurrent connections, is a common choice for high-performance websites. It's essential to configure your web server for optimal performance, including setting up caching mechanisms and fine-tuning server settings.

5. Caching

Caching involves storing frequently accessed data in memory for quick retrieval, reducing the need to regenerate content on every request. Implement server-side caching mechanisms such as object caching (for database queries), opcode caching (for PHP), and page caching (for entire web pages). WordPress, for example, offers various caching plugins like W3 Total Cache and WP Super Cache.

6. Load Balancing

For high-traffic websites, load balancing distributes incoming traffic across multiple servers to prevent overload and ensure high availability. Services like Amazon Elastic Load Balancing (ELB) and HAProxy can help implement load balancing efficiently.

7. Database Optimization

Database queries can be a bottleneck for server performance. Optimize your database by:

- Indexing database tables for faster data retrieval.
- Reducing unnecessary database queries and optimizing SQL queries.
- Implementing database caching to store query results.

8. Minimize HTTP Requests

Reducing the number of HTTP requests required to load a web page can significantly improve performance. Combine CSS and JavaScript files, use image sprites, and minimize the use of external resources to minimize HTTP requests.

9. Regular Software Updates

Keep your server's operating system, web server software, and other components up to date. Updates often include security fixes and performance improvements.

10. Monitoring and Scaling

Regularly monitor your server's performance using tools like New Relic, Nagios, or Prometheus. When traffic increases, be prepared to scale your server resources horizontally (adding more servers) or vertically (upgrading server resources).

In conclusion, server-side performance optimization is a continuous process that requires careful planning, monitoring, and fine-tuning. By choosing the right hosting plan, optimizing server hardware and resources, implementing CDNs and caching, and following best practices, you can ensure that your website delivers a fast and reliable user experience. Regular maintenance and monitoring are essential to address performance issues promptly and keep your website running smoothly.

Chapter 18: Web Analytics and User Experience

Section 18.1: Analyzing User Behavior with Analytics

In the realm of web design and development, understanding user behavior is paramount for creating successful websites. To gain insights into how users interact with your site, web analytics tools play a pivotal role. In this section, we will explore the significance of web analytics and delve into techniques for analyzing user behavior.

Why Web Analytics Matter

1. **Data-Driven Decisions:** Web analytics provides quantitative data about your website's performance, helping you make informed decisions. You can identify which pages are popular, track user journeys, and measure the effectiveness of your design and content.

2. **User Engagement:** Analytics tools help you assess user engagement metrics like bounce rate, session duration, and page views. These metrics indicate how well your site captures and retains user attention.

3. **Conversion Tracking:** If your website has specific goals such as sign-ups, purchases, or form submissions, analytics can track conversions. This information is crucial for optimizing your site's conversion rate.

4. **Content Optimization:** Analytics tools reveal which content resonates with your audience. By analyzing popular pages and blog posts, you can create more of the content that your users find valuable.

Key Metrics to Monitor

1. **Pageviews:** The total number of pages viewed by users on your site. It's a basic indicator of site traffic.

2. **Bounce Rate:** The percentage of visitors who leave your site after viewing only one page. A high bounce rate may indicate issues with your landing pages.

3. **Session Duration:** The average amount of time users spend on your site during a session. Longer sessions often correlate with engaged users.

4. **Conversion Rate:** The percentage of visitors who complete a desired action, such as making a purchase or signing up for a newsletter.

5. **Traffic Sources:** Analytics tools categorize traffic into sources like organic search, direct, referral, and social. Understanding these sources helps you identify which marketing channels are most effective.

Popular Analytics Tools

1. **Google Analytics:** A widely used, free analytics tool that provides comprehensive data on user behavior, traffic sources, and more.

2. **Hotjar:** Offers heatmaps, session recordings, and surveys to visualize user interactions and feedback.

3. **Mixpanel:** Focuses on user-based analytics, helping you understand individual user behavior and track their journeys.

4. **Heap:** Allows retroactive tracking of user interactions, making it easy to set up and analyze events without prior configuration.

Implementing Analytics

To get started with web analytics:

1. **Sign Up:** Create an account with your chosen analytics tool (e.g., Google Analytics) and obtain a tracking code snippet.

2. **Integration:** Add the tracking code to your website's HTML, usually just before the closing </head> tag on each page.

3. **Goals and Events:** Set up goals or events to track specific user actions, such as completing a purchase or submitting a contact form.

4. **Customization:** Tailor your analytics setup to focus on the metrics that matter most to your website's objectives.

5. **Regular Analysis:** Periodically review your analytics data to identify trends, areas for improvement, and opportunities for optimization.

In conclusion, web analytics is a powerful tool for understanding user behavior and improving your website's performance. By monitoring key metrics, using the right analytics tools, and implementing tracking codes effectively, you can make data-driven decisions and create a better user experience. Understanding your audience's needs and preferences is essential for achieving web design success.

Section 18.2: Heatmaps and User Session Recording

In the realm of web analytics and user experience (UX) research, heatmaps and user session recording tools are invaluable resources. They provide visual insights into how users interact with your website, allowing you to pinpoint areas for improvement and enhance the overall user experience. In this section, we will explore heatmaps and user session recording in detail.

Heatmaps

Heatmaps are graphical representations of user interactions on a web page. They use color coding to indicate where users click, move their mouse, or scroll. Here's a breakdown of the types of heatmaps commonly used:

1. **Click Heatmaps:** These heatmaps show where users click most frequently on a web page. Clicks are represented by different colors, with hotspots indicating areas of high interaction.

2. **Move Heatmaps:** Move heatmaps track mouse movement. They reveal where users hover their cursors, providing insights into areas of interest or confusion.

3. **Scroll Heatmaps:** Scroll heatmaps illustrate how far users typically scroll down a page. Understanding where users drop off can help you optimize content placement.

4. **Attention Heatmaps:** These combine click, move, and scroll data to create an overall attention heatmap. They highlight the areas where users focus their attention the most.

Use Cases for Heatmaps

- **Identifying Dead Zones:** Heatmaps can reveal parts of a web page that receive little to no interaction. This information helps in optimizing layouts and content placement.

- **Validating Design Changes:** After making design modifications, heatmaps can confirm whether the changes have positively impacted user engagement.

- **Improving Call to Action (CTA) Buttons:** By analyzing click heatmaps, you can determine whether CTAs are well-positioned and effective.

User Session Recording

User session recording tools capture and replay real user interactions on your website. They record mouse movements, clicks, keystrokes, and even user sessions with multiple page views. This allows you to see exactly how individual users navigate your site.

Benefits of User Session Recording

1. **Bugs and Issues:** User session recordings are excellent for identifying usability issues, bugs, or glitches that users encounter.

2. **User Behavior:** By watching how users interact with your site, you can gain deeper insights into their behavior, pain points, and preferences.

3. **User Testing:** Session recordings can be valuable for user testing and UX research. They provide direct feedback on design and usability.

4. **Conversion Optimization:** You can pinpoint where users drop off in the conversion funnel and make targeted improvements to boost conversion rates.

Implementing Heatmaps and Session Recording

To implement heatmaps and user session recording on your website:

1. **Choose a Tool:** There are various tools available, such as Hotjar, Crazy Egg, and Mouseflow. Select one that suits your needs and budget.

2. **Integration:** Sign up for the chosen tool and integrate it into your website. This often involves adding a code snippet to your site's HTML.

3. **Configuration:** Configure the tool to track the specific types of data you want to collect (e.g., click, move, scroll, or user sessions).

4. **Privacy Considerations:** Be mindful of user privacy and ensure your implementation complies with relevant data protection regulations, such as GDPR or CCPA.

5. **Analysis:** Regularly review the heatmap and session recording data to gain insights and inform design and content decisions.

In conclusion, heatmaps and user session recording tools are indispensable for understanding user behavior, optimizing website design, and enhancing the user experience. By leveraging these tools, web designers and developers can make data-driven decisions that lead to more engaging and user-friendly websites.

Section 18.3: A/B Testing and Conversion Optimization

A/B testing, also known as split testing, is a powerful technique in web analytics and optimization. It allows you to compare two or more versions of a web page to determine which one performs better in terms of achieving a specific goal. In this section, we'll explore A/B testing and its role in conversion optimization.

Understanding A/B Testing

A/B testing involves creating two (or more) versions of a web page: the original (A) and one or more variations (B, C, etc.). These variations contain changes to elements such as headlines, images, buttons, layouts, or any other aspect of the page that might impact user behavior.

The primary objective of A/B testing is to understand how these changes affect user behavior and performance metrics, such as click-through rates, conversion rates, or revenue. By collecting data from real users, you can make informed decisions about which version of the page is more effective.

Steps in A/B Testing

1. **Goal Identification:** Define a specific goal for your A/B test. It could be increasing the click-through rate on a call-to-action (CTA) button, improving the conversion rate of a signup form, or enhancing the engagement with a product page.

2. **Creation of Variations:** Create the different versions of your web page. For instance, if you're testing a CTA button, you might create variations with different text, colors, or placements.

3. **Randomization:** Users are randomly assigned to see either the original (A) or one of the variations (B, C, etc.). This randomization is crucial to ensure unbiased results.

4. **Data Collection:** Collect data on user interactions and conversions for each group over a predefined period. Use analytics tools or A/B testing platforms to track these metrics.

5. **Statistical Analysis:** Analyze the data to determine which variation performed better based on your defined goal. Statistical significance is essential to ensure that the results are meaningful.

6. **Implementation of Winning Variation:** If one of the variations significantly outperforms the others, implement it as the new version of your web page.

Benefits of A/B Testing

- **Data-Driven Decisions:** A/B testing provides empirical evidence of what changes positively impact user behavior, allowing you to make informed decisions based on real user interactions.

- **Continuous Improvement:** It promotes a culture of continuous improvement by encouraging iterative testing and refinement of web elements.

- **Risk Mitigation:** Rather than making substantial design or content changes based on assumptions, A/B testing minimizes risk by validating changes through experimentation.

- **Personalization:** A/B testing can be used to create personalized experiences for different segments of your audience, optimizing the user journey for various user groups.

Tips for Successful A/B Testing

1. **Focus on One Variable:** Test one element at a time (e.g., a single CTA button change) to isolate the impact of that change.

2. **Sufficient Sample Size:** Ensure you have a sufficiently large sample size to draw statistically significant conclusions.

3. **Test for a Sufficient Duration:** Run tests for an adequate duration to account for variations in user behavior over time, considering seasonality and other factors.

4. **Document and Learn:** Keep detailed records of your A/B tests, including the variations tested, results, and lessons learned. This knowledge can inform future optimization efforts.

5. **Iterate and Repeat:** A/B testing should be an ongoing process. As you make improvements, continue testing to refine your website further.

In conclusion, A/B testing is a valuable technique for optimizing web pages and achieving specific goals. By scientifically testing variations and measuring their impact on user behavior, web designers and marketers can make data-backed decisions that lead to improved website performance and better user experiences.

Section 18.4: Usability Testing and User-Centered Design

Usability testing is a critical component of user-centered design (UCD), a methodology that prioritizes the needs and preferences of users throughout the design and development process. In this section, we will explore the importance of usability testing and how it contributes to creating user-friendly websites and applications.

Understanding Usability Testing

Usability testing involves observing real users as they interact with a website or application to evaluate its ease of use and effectiveness in achieving its intended goals. The primary purpose is to identify usability issues, gather user feedback, and make informed design improvements.

Key aspects of usability testing include:

1. **User-Centered Approach:** Usability testing is centered around the needs, preferences, and behaviors of the target audience. It helps ensure that a website or application aligns with user expectations.

2. **Real Users:** Usability tests involve real users who represent the target audience. Their interactions and feedback provide valuable insights into how well the design meets user needs.

3. **Objective Evaluation:** Usability testing is objective, focusing on concrete aspects like task completion rates, time on task, error rates, and user satisfaction.

4. **Iterative Process:** Usability testing is typically an iterative process, meaning that designers and developers make improvements based on test results and then retest to validate the changes.

Benefits of Usability Testing

Usability testing offers numerous benefits:

- **Identification of Pain Points:** Usability tests uncover pain points and usability issues that may not be apparent through other methods. These issues can range from confusing navigation to unclear instructions.

- **Improved User Satisfaction:** By addressing usability issues, you can enhance the overall user experience, leading to increased user satisfaction and loyalty.

- **Enhanced Efficiency:** Usability improvements often result in more efficient task completion, which is essential for websites and applications aimed at productivity.

- **Reduced Development Costs:** Identifying and resolving usability issues early in the design phase can save development costs associated with making significant changes later.

- **Competitive Advantage:** A user-centered approach that prioritizes usability can give your website or application a competitive edge in the market.

Conducting Usability Testing

Here are the general steps to conduct usability testing:

1. **Define Objectives:** Clearly define the goals and objectives of the usability test. What specific tasks or interactions do you want to evaluate?

2. **Recruit Participants:** Identify and recruit participants who represent your target audience. Consider factors like age, experience level, and demographics.

3. **Create Test Scenarios:** Develop scenarios or tasks that participants will perform during the test. These tasks should align with the objectives and represent common user interactions.

4. **Conduct the Test:** Observe participants as they complete the tasks while providing minimal guidance. Encourage them to think aloud, expressing their thoughts and reactions.

5. **Collect Data:** Record data on task completion rates, time on task, errors, and user feedback. This data will be used to evaluate the usability of the design.

6. **Analyze Results:** Analyze the data to identify usability issues and areas for improvement. Categorize issues by severity and prioritize them for resolution.

7. **Iterate and Redesign:** Make design changes based on the findings and retest the design to verify the improvements.

Usability Testing Tools

There are various usability testing tools and platforms available that can help streamline the testing process. These tools often provide features for remote testing, screen recording, and real-time user feedback collection. Some popular usability testing tools include UsabilityHub, UserTesting, and Optimal Workshop.

In conclusion, usability testing is a fundamental part of user-centered design, ensuring that websites and applications meet the needs and expectations of their users. By identifying and addressing usability issues, designers and developers can create more user-friendly and effective digital experiences.

Section 18.5: Feedback and Continuous Improvement

Feedback plays a pivotal role in the ongoing improvement of web design and user experience. In this section, we'll explore the significance of feedback and how it contributes to the iterative enhancement of websites and applications.

The Importance of Feedback

Feedback is a valuable source of information that allows designers and developers to understand how users perceive and interact with their digital products. It provides insights into what works well and what needs improvement. Here are key reasons why feedback is crucial:

1. **User-Centered Perspective:** Feedback brings the user's perspective into focus, helping designers align their creations with user needs and preferences.

2. **Identification of Issues:** Feedback helps identify usability issues, bugs, or design flaws that may have been overlooked during development.

3. **Validation of Design Choices:** It validates design decisions and informs whether the intended message or functionality is effectively communicated to users.

4. **User Satisfaction:** Gathering feedback and acting on it can lead to improved user satisfaction, loyalty, and retention.

5. **Competitive Advantage:** Responding to user feedback can give a website or application a competitive edge by addressing pain points and delivering a superior user experience.

Feedback Collection Methods

There are various methods for collecting feedback from users:

1. **Surveys:** Online surveys can be used to gather structured feedback on specific aspects of a website or application. Tools like Google Forms or SurveyMonkey make it easy to create and distribute surveys.

2. **User Testing:** As discussed in previous sections, user testing involves observing users while they interact with your product. This method provides detailed insights into user behavior and preferences.

3. **Feedback Forms:** Include feedback forms on your website or app, allowing users to provide comments, suggestions, and report issues. Ensure that these forms are easily accessible and user-friendly.

4. **Analytics Tools:** Web analytics tools like Google Analytics provide data on user behavior, page views, and more. Analyzing this data can help identify areas that require attention.

5. **Social Media and Reviews:** Monitor social media channels and user reviews to gain insights into how users are discussing your product. Responding to comments and reviews can also demonstrate responsiveness.

Managing feedback effectively is as important as collecting it. Here are some tips:

1. **Prioritize Feedback:** Categorize feedback based on severity and impact. Focus on addressing critical issues first.

2. **Create an Internal Feedback Loop:** Ensure that feedback reaches the relevant teams or individuals responsible for design and development.

3. **Acknowledge and Respond:** Acknowledge user feedback promptly, even if it's to thank users for their input. When issues are resolved, communicate the changes made.

4. **Regular Review:** Schedule regular reviews of user feedback to identify recurring issues and trends.

5. **Iterative Improvement:** Use feedback to inform iterative design and development processes. Continuously work on enhancing the user experience.

6. **User-Centered Design:** Keep user feedback at the forefront of design decisions. Involve users in the design process whenever possible.

Leveraging Feedback for Continuous Improvement

Feedback is not a one-time effort but a continuous cycle of improvement. By actively seeking and acting on user feedback, web designers and developers can create products that are better aligned with user expectations, more user-friendly, and ultimately more successful. It's a practice that ensures your digital presence evolves alongside the changing needs and preferences of your audience.

Chapter 19: Building E-Commerce Websites

In this chapter, we will delve into the essential aspects of creating e-commerce websites. E-commerce has become a significant part of the online business landscape, and understanding how to design and develop e-commerce platforms is crucial for success in the digital marketplace.

Section 19.1: E-Commerce Website Essentials

E-commerce websites are online platforms that enable businesses to sell products or services directly to customers over the internet. These websites have unique requirements and challenges compared to informational or corporate websites. In this section, we will explore the fundamental elements and considerations for building an effective e-commerce website.

1. *Product Listings and Catalogs:*
   - **Product Pages:** Each product should have a dedicated page with detailed information, high-quality images, pricing, and an "Add to Cart" button.
   - **Product Categories:** Organize products into categories and subcategories to help users navigate and find what they're looking for.
   - **Search Functionality:** Implement a robust search feature that allows users to search by keywords, filters, and attributes.

2. *Shopping Cart and Checkout:*
   - **Shopping Cart:** Enable users to add products to their cart, view cart contents, and proceed to checkout.
   - **Checkout Process:** Streamline the checkout process with as few steps as possible. Include shipping and payment options.
   - **Guest Checkout:** Offer a guest checkout option for users who don't want to create an account.

3. *User Accounts and Authentication:*
   - **User Registration:** Allow users to create accounts for easy access to order history and saved information.
   - **Login and Security:** Implement secure authentication and password recovery processes.
   - **Personalization:** Use user accounts to provide personalized recommendations and offers.

4. *Payment Processing:*
   - **Payment Gateways:** Integrate secure payment gateways like PayPal, Stripe, or others to facilitate online transactions.
   - **Security:** Ensure the highest level of security for handling sensitive payment information.

5. *Shipping and Delivery:*
   - **Shipping Options:** Offer various shipping methods, including express, standard, and international shipping.
   - **Tracking:** Provide shipment tracking information to keep customers informed about their orders.

6. *Product Reviews and Ratings:*
   - **User Reviews:** Allow customers to leave reviews and ratings for products.
   - **Trust Building:** Display reviews and ratings prominently to build trust among potential buyers.

7. Security and Privacy:

- **SSL Certificate:** Use SSL certificates to encrypt data transmission and protect customer information.
- **Privacy Policy:** Clearly communicate how customer data is handled and protected in a privacy policy.

8. Responsive Design:

- **Mobile Optimization:** Ensure the website is responsive and optimized for mobile devices to reach a broader audience.

9. Performance Optimization:

- **Page Speed:** Optimize website performance for fast loading times to reduce bounce rates and improve user experience.
- **Scalability:** Ensure the website can handle increased traffic during promotions and sales events.

10. Legal Compliance:

- **Terms and Conditions:** Include clear terms and conditions for using the website and making purchases.
- **Return Policy:** Specify the return and refund policies.

Building an e-commerce website involves careful planning, development, and ongoing maintenance. In the following sections, we will delve deeper into specific aspects of e-commerce, including payment integration, product recommendations, and security measures.

Section 19.2: Shopping Carts and Payment Integration

Shopping carts and payment integration are fundamental components of any e-commerce website. In this section, we will explore the key considerations and best practices for implementing shopping carts and integrating payment gateways into your online store.

Shopping Cart Functionality

1. Adding Products to the Cart:

- A user should be able to easily add products to their shopping cart from product pages. This typically involves a prominent "Add to Cart" button.

2. Cart Contents and Summary:

- Display the contents of the user's cart, including product names, quantities, prices, and a subtotal. Provide the option to update quantities or remove items.

3. Cart Persistence:

- Ensure that the cart retains its contents even if the user logs out or leaves the website. This is achieved by using cookies or user accounts.

4. Cross-Selling and Upselling:

- Implement features that suggest related or complementary products to encourage users to add more items to their cart.

5. Clear Call to Action:

- Use clear and persuasive calls to action (CTAs) to guide users through the checkout process, such as "Proceed to Checkout" or "Continue Shopping."

Checkout Process

1. Streamlined Checkout:

- Keep the checkout process as simple and efficient as possible. Ideally, it should be a few steps, including shipping, payment, and order confirmation.

2. Guest Checkout:

- Offer the option for users to check out as guests, without requiring them to create an account. This reduces friction for first-time customers.

3. Shipping Options:

- Provide various shipping options, including express, standard, and international shipping. Clearly communicate delivery times and costs.

4. Billing and Shipping Information:

- Collect billing and shipping information accurately. Implement address validation to prevent errors.

5. Payment Methods:

- Offer a variety of payment methods, including credit/debit cards, digital wallets (e.g., PayPal, Apple Pay), and alternative payment options.

Payment Integration

1. Secure Payment Gateways:

- Integrate trusted and secure payment gateways that encrypt sensitive payment information. Common choices include PayPal, Stripe, and Square.

2. SSL Encryption:

- Ensure your website uses SSL encryption to protect data transmitted between the user's browser and your server during the payment process.

3. PCI Compliance:

- Comply with Payment Card Industry Data Security Standard (PCI DSS) requirements to safeguard credit card data.

4. Payment Confirmation:

- Provide users with a clear payment confirmation page and email receipt. Include order details and a unique order ID.

5. Error Handling:

- Implement error handling for failed transactions and communicate errors to users with helpful messages.

6. Testing and Debugging:

- Thoroughly test the payment process, including test transactions, to ensure that it works seamlessly without issues.

7. Refund and Cancellation Policies:

- Clearly communicate refund and cancellation policies to users during the checkout process.

Remember that trust and security are paramount in e-commerce. Users need to feel confident that their payment information is safe, and the checkout process is hassle-free. By following best practices and using reputable payment gateways, you can create a positive shopping experience for your customers.

Section 19.3: Product Catalogs and Search Functionality

A well-structured product catalog and robust search functionality are vital components of an e-commerce website. In this section, we will delve into the key considerations for creating and managing a product catalog and implementing effective search features.

Creating a Product Catalog

1. Product Information:

- Collect comprehensive product information, including product names, descriptions, prices, images, and specifications. Ensure that product details are accurate and up-to-date.

2. Categorization:

- Organize products into categories and subcategories for easy navigation. Use a logical and intuitive structure that aligns with your target audience's preferences.

3. Product Variations:

- If your products come in different variations (e.g., sizes, colors), create separate listings or product pages for each variation with clear options for selection.

4. Product Attributes:

- Define attributes (e.g., brand, material, size) that users can use to filter and refine their product searches. Assign attributes consistently across your catalog.

5. Product Availability:

- Clearly indicate the availability status of each product, whether it's in stock, out of stock, or available for pre-order.

6. *Product Reviews and Ratings:*
- Allow customers to leave reviews and ratings for products. Display these ratings prominently to build trust and assist other shoppers in making decisions.

Implementing Search Functionality

1. *Search Bar Placement:*
- Place the search bar prominently, usually at the top of every page, to make it easily accessible to users.

2. *Auto-Suggestions:*
- Implement auto-suggestions that appear as users type their queries. This can help users find products faster and correct potential misspellings.

3. *Filters and Sorting:*
- Provide robust filtering and sorting options, allowing users to refine search results based on attributes (e.g., price range, brand, rating) and sort by relevance, price, or popularity.

4. *Search Results Page:*
- Design a clean and informative search results page that displays product thumbnails, names, prices, and brief descriptions. Ensure that users can see how their search query matches the results.

5. *No Results Handling:*
- When a search query returns no results, display a clear message and suggest alternative searches or popular products.

6. *Pagination and Infinite Scroll:*
- Implement pagination or infinite scroll on the search results page to accommodate a large number of products and enhance user experience.

7. *Mobile Optimization:*
- Ensure that your search functionality is mobile-friendly, as many users shop on smartphones and tablets.

Managing Product Data

1. *Inventory Management:*
- Keep accurate track of your inventory to prevent overselling or listing out-of-stock products.

2. *Regular Updates:*
- Regularly update your product catalog with new arrivals, discontinued items, and changes in product details.

3. SEO Optimization:

- Optimize product descriptions and metadata for search engines to improve organic visibility.

4. Product Images:

- Use high-quality images for products, with multiple angles and zoom functionality to allow users to examine products closely.

5. Cross-Selling:

- Implement cross-selling strategies by suggesting related products on product pages to encourage additional purchases.

6. User Feedback:

- Listen to user feedback and monitor user behavior to make continuous improvements to your product catalog and search functionality.

A well-curated product catalog and effective search features can significantly impact the user experience on your e-commerce site. Ensuring that users can easily find and explore your products will lead to higher conversion rates and customer satisfaction. Regularly maintaining and optimizing your product catalog is essential to keeping your online store competitive and user-friendly.

Section 19.4: User Accounts and Authentication

User accounts and authentication are fundamental aspects of e-commerce websites. In this section, we will explore the importance of user accounts, how to implement user registration and login, and best practices for user authentication.

The Importance of User Accounts

User accounts serve several essential purposes in e-commerce:

1. **Personalization:** User accounts allow you to personalize the shopping experience. You can recommend products based on user behavior and preferences.

2. **Order History:** Users can view their order history, making it easier to track past purchases, reorder items, and review receipts.

3. **Saved Information:** Users can store their shipping addresses and payment details, streamlining the checkout process.

4. **Wishlists:** Users can create wishlists to save products for later and receive notifications about price drops or availability.

5. **Reviews and Ratings:** Registered users can leave product reviews and ratings, contributing to your site's credibility.

Implementing User Registration

1. Registration Form:
- Create a user-friendly registration form that collects essential information, such as name, email address, and password.

2. Password Requirements:
- Enforce password requirements, such as minimum length, a mix of uppercase and lowercase letters, numbers, and special characters. Encourage users to create strong passwords.

3. Email Verification:
- Implement email verification to ensure that users provide a valid email address. Send a verification link to the user's email to confirm their registration.

4. CAPTCHA and Security:
- Use CAPTCHA or other anti-bot measures to prevent automated registration. This enhances security and prevents spam accounts.

User Authentication

1. Login Page:
- Design a user-friendly login page that allows registered users to enter their credentials securely.

2. Remember Me:
- Provide a "Remember Me" option for users who want to stay logged in on their trusted devices.

3. Password Reset:
- Implement a "Forgot Password" feature that allows users to reset their passwords via email. Ensure that the reset process is secure.

4. Session Management:
- Manage user sessions securely. Implement session timeouts and ensure that sessions expire after a period of inactivity.

Best Practices for User Authentication

1. Use HTTPS:
- Always use HTTPS to encrypt data transmitted between the user's browser and your server. An SSL certificate is crucial for securing user information.

2. Hashed Passwords:
- Store user passwords securely by hashing and salting them before saving in the database. Never store plain-text passwords.

3. Two-Factor Authentication (2FA):

- Encourage users to enable 2FA for an extra layer of security. This typically involves receiving a one-time code on their mobile device.

4. Account Lockout:

- Implement account lockout mechanisms to prevent brute-force attacks. After a certain number of failed login attempts, lock the account temporarily.

5. Data Protection Compliance:

- Ensure that your authentication process complies with data protection regulations like GDPR or CCPA. Be transparent about data usage and obtain user consent where necessary.

6. Security Audits:

- Regularly conduct security audits and vulnerability assessments to identify and address potential weaknesses in your authentication system.

User accounts and authentication play a pivotal role in the trust and security of your e-commerce platform. By implementing best practices and ensuring a seamless user experience during registration and login, you can build and maintain customer trust while safeguarding their sensitive information.

Section 19.5: Security Considerations in E-Commerce

Ensuring the security of an e-commerce website is paramount to protect both your business and your customers. In this section, we will delve into various security considerations that every e-commerce site should address to mitigate risks and maintain trust.

Data Encryption

Data encryption is a fundamental security measure in e-commerce. It involves encoding sensitive information like credit card details and personal data to prevent unauthorized access during transmission. The primary encryption protocol used for this purpose is Secure Sockets Layer (SSL) or its successor, Transport Layer Security (TLS). To implement data encryption:

1. **SSL/TLS Certificates:** Obtain an SSL/TLS certificate for your domain. This certificate ensures that data transmitted between your website and users' browsers is encrypted.

2. **HTTPS:** Configure your web server to use HTTPS. This ensures that your website is accessible via a secure, encrypted connection. Always display a padlock icon in the browser's address bar to signal a secure connection to users.

Payment Card Industry Data Security Standard (PCI DSS) Compliance

If your e-commerce site handles credit card transactions, compliance with the PCI DSS is mandatory. PCI DSS outlines security requirements to protect cardholder data. Key aspects of PCI DSS compliance include:

1. **Secure Payment Processing:** Ensure that payment processing is secure, and card data is not stored on your servers.

2. **Regular Security Audits:** Conduct regular security audits and assessments to identify vulnerabilities and address them promptly.

3. **Access Control:** Implement strict access controls to limit access to cardholder data to authorized personnel only.

Regular Security Audits

Regular security audits and vulnerability assessments are essential to identify and address potential weaknesses in your e-commerce platform. These assessments can include penetration testing, code reviews, and security scanning tools. Consider the following aspects:

1. **Penetration Testing:** Hire security professionals to perform penetration tests to identify vulnerabilities that could be exploited by attackers.

2. **Code Reviews:** Conduct thorough code reviews to ensure that your web application's code follows best security practices. Address any issues or vulnerabilities discovered during these reviews.

3. **Security Scanning Tools:** Use automated security scanning tools to detect common vulnerabilities like SQL injection, cross-site scripting (XSS), and cross-site request forgery (CSRF).

DDoS Mitigation

Distributed Denial of Service (DDoS) attacks can disrupt your e-commerce site's availability and impact your business. To mitigate DDoS attacks:

1. **Content Delivery Network (CDN):** Use a CDN to distribute website content across multiple servers and data centers. CDNs can absorb traffic spikes and mitigate DDoS attacks.

2. **Web Application Firewall (WAF):** Implement a WAF to filter and block malicious traffic before it reaches your web servers.

User Data Protection

Protecting customer data is crucial for maintaining trust. Follow these practices:

1. **Data Minimization:** Collect and store only the data necessary for transactions. Avoid retaining sensitive information longer than required.

2. **User Consent:** Clearly inform users about data usage and obtain their consent for activities like storing payment information.

3. **Data Encryption at Rest:** Encrypt stored user data, including personal details and payment information, to protect against data breaches.

Incident Response Plan

Prepare an incident response plan to address security breaches or data leaks promptly. Your plan should include:

1. **Notification Procedures:** Define how and when to notify affected users and relevant authorities in case of a data breach.

2. **Containment and Recovery:** Outline steps to contain the breach, recover lost data, and restore normal operations.

3. **Legal and Regulatory Compliance:** Ensure that your response plan complies with legal and regulatory requirements regarding data breaches.

4. **Communication:** Designate a spokesperson and create communication templates for addressing the media and customers during a breach.

5. **Post-Incident Evaluation:** After an incident, conduct a post-incident evaluation to identify lessons learned and improve your security measures.

Ongoing Security Awareness

Maintain a culture of security awareness among your team members. Provide training and raise awareness about the latest security threats and best practices. Encourage employees to report security concerns promptly.

By addressing these security considerations, you can bolster the security of your e-commerce website, protect customer data, and maintain the trust and confidence of your users. Keep in mind that security is an ongoing process, and staying vigilant is essential in the ever-evolving landscape of cybersecurity.

Chapter 20: Web Design Trends and Future Directions

In this final chapter, we will explore the ever-evolving landscape of web design, including current trends and future directions that are shaping the industry. Web design is a dynamic field, influenced by changes in technology, user behavior, and emerging design philosophies. Staying updated on these trends is essential for web designers and developers to create innovative and user-centric web experiences.

Section 20.1: Emerging Web Technologies

WebAssembly (Wasm)

WebAssembly (Wasm) is a binary instruction format that allows high-performance execution of code on web browsers. It enables developers to run applications at near-native speed directly within web pages. This technology opens up new possibilities for building web applications, including games, video editing tools, and even complex simulations. Wasm is becoming increasingly popular and is supported by major browsers like Chrome, Firefox, Edge, and Safari.

Example: Using WebAssembly

```javascript
// WebAssembly Module
const wasmModule = new WebAssembly.Module(Uint8Array.of(0x00, 0x61, 0x73,
0x6D, 0x01, 0x00, 0x00, 0x00));

// WebAssembly Instance
const wasmInstance = new WebAssembly.Instance(wasmModule);

// Calling a WebAssembly function
const result = wasmInstance.exports.add(2, 3);
console.log(result); // Output: 5
```

Web Components

Web Components are a set of web platform APIs that allow you to create custom, reusable, and encapsulated HTML elements. They consist of three main technologies: Custom Elements, Shadow DOM, and HTML Templates. Web Components promote modular development and can be used with any web framework or library. They are gaining traction for building components that work seamlessly across different projects.

Example: Creating a Custom Element

```javascript
class MyCustomElement extends HTMLElement {
  constructor() {
    super();
    // Define the shadow DOM for encapsulation
    const shadow = this.attachShadow({ mode: 'open' });
    // Create a new paragraph element
```

```
    const paragraph = document.createElement('p');
    paragraph.textContent = 'This is my custom element!';
    // Append the paragraph to the shadow DOM
    shadow.appendChild(paragraph);
  }
}

// Register the custom element
customElements.define('my-custom-element', MyCustomElement);
```

WebAssembly and Web Components Integration

WebAssembly and Web Components can be used together to create powerful, efficient, and modular web applications. WebAssembly can handle performance-critical tasks, while Web Components provide a clean and encapsulated way to structure the user interface. This combination allows developers to build complex web applications that are both fast and maintainable.

Conclusion

Web design continues to evolve, driven by technological advancements and changing user expectations. Embracing emerging technologies like WebAssembly and Web Components can empower web designers and developers to create web experiences that are faster, more modular, and more engaging. As the web landscape evolves, staying curious and adaptable will be key to success in the field of web design.

This concludes our journey through the world of web design. We hope this book has provided you with valuable insights, skills, and inspiration to excel in this dynamic and creative field. Remember that web design is a blend of art and technology, and your creativity combined with a strong foundation in web design principles will enable you to craft exceptional web experiences.

Section 20.2: Progressive Web Apps (PWAs)

Progressive Web Apps (PWAs) represent a significant shift in the way web applications are developed and delivered. They are web applications that leverage modern web technologies to provide an app-like experience to users, regardless of the device or platform they are using. PWAs are designed to be fast, reliable, and engaging, combining the best features of web and mobile applications.

Key Characteristics of PWAs

1. **Responsive:** PWAs are built to work seamlessly on any device, from desktops to smartphones and tablets. They adapt to different screen sizes and orientations.

2. **Offline Capabilities:** One of the defining features of PWAs is their ability to work offline or in low-network conditions. Service Workers, a script that runs in the background, enable this functionality by caching essential assets and data.

3. **App-Like Experience:** PWAs are designed to feel like native mobile apps. They offer smooth animations, fluid navigation, and intuitive interactions, making them user-friendly.

4. **Installation-Free:** Unlike traditional apps, PWAs do not require installation from an app store. Users can simply visit a PWA-enabled website and add it to their home screen if they wish.

5. **Up-to-Date:** PWAs are always up-to-date, as they automatically fetch the latest version when connected to the internet. This eliminates the need for users to manually update the app.

Building a PWA

To create a Progressive Web App, several key components and technologies are typically involved:

- **Service Workers:** These are JavaScript files that run in the background, intercepting network requests, and caching resources to provide offline functionality.

- **Web App Manifest:** This JSON file defines metadata about the app, such as its name, icons, and start URL. It helps browsers understand how to display the app when installed on a user's device.

- **HTTPS:** PWAs require a secure HTTPS connection to ensure the integrity and security of data being transferred between the user's device and the server.

Example of a Web App Manifest:

```json
{
  "name": "My PWA",
  "short_name": "PWA",
  "description": "A progressive web app example",
  "start_url": "/",
  "display": "standalone",
  "background_color": "#ffffff",
  "theme_color": "#000000",
  "icons": [
    {
      "src": "/images/icon.png",
      "sizes": "192x192",
      "type": "image/png"
    }
  ]
}
```

Benefits of PWAs

PWAs offer several advantages for both developers and users:

- **Cross-Platform Compatibility:** PWAs work on various platforms, reducing the need for separate development for different operating systems.

- **Improved Performance:** Service Workers cache resources, making PWAs faster to load and reducing server load.

- **Lower Development Costs:** Developing a single PWA can be more cost-effective than building separate native apps for iOS and Android.

- **User Engagement:** PWAs can send push notifications, increasing user engagement and retention.

- **Accessibility:** PWAs are accessible to a wide range of users, including those with slower internet connections or older devices.

PWAs in the Future

As technology continues to evolve, PWAs are likely to become even more prominent. They align with the trend toward web-based solutions and the desire for faster, more user-friendly experiences. With advancements in web APIs and browser capabilities, PWAs will play a crucial role in the future of web application development, offering users a reliable and engaging way to interact with online services.

Section 20.3: Voice User Interfaces (VUIs)

Voice User Interfaces (VUIs) represent a significant shift in how users interact with technology and access information. These interfaces allow users to interact with devices, applications, and services using spoken language. The rise of voice assistants like Amazon's Alexa, Google Assistant, and Apple's Siri has propelled VUIs into the mainstream, making them an essential consideration for web designers and developers.

The Growth of VUIs

The popularity of VUIs can be attributed to several factors:

1. **Accessibility:** VUIs are highly accessible to a wide range of users, including those with disabilities or limited mobility. They offer an inclusive way to interact with technology.

2. **Convenience:** Voice commands are often faster and more convenient than typing or navigating through menus. Users can get answers and perform tasks quickly.

3. **Natural Interaction:** Speaking is a natural form of communication, making VUIs intuitive for many users, including those who may not be tech-savvy.

4. **Hands-Free Operation:** VUIs enable hands-free operation, which is particularly valuable in situations where manual interaction with devices or screens is impractical or unsafe.

When designing for VUIs, several considerations come into play:

- **Voice Commands:** Designers must identify the most common voice commands users are likely to use and ensure that the VUI understands and responds appropriately.

- **Context Awareness:** VUIs should be context-aware, allowing users to have natural, multi-turn conversations. They should remember previous interactions to provide a seamless experience.

- **Error Handling:** It's crucial to design effective error handling and recovery mechanisms, as users may phrase requests in various ways or encounter misunderstandings.

- **Personalization:** VUIs can be personalized to individual users, providing tailored responses and recommendations based on user preferences and history.

- **Multimodal Interfaces:** Some VUIs support multimodal interfaces, allowing users to combine voice commands with touch, gestures, or visual elements.

Challenges of VUI Design

While VUIs offer many advantages, they also present unique challenges for designers and developers:

- **Speech Recognition Accuracy:** Achieving high speech recognition accuracy, especially for multiple languages and accents, can be challenging.

- **Privacy and Security:** Voice data is sensitive, and designers must prioritize privacy and security to protect user information.

- **Limited Screen Real Estate:** VUIs typically have limited screen space for displaying information, requiring careful consideration of what and how information is presented.

- **Testing and Feedback:** Usability testing for VUIs may require different approaches than traditional UI testing, as voice interactions are more difficult to simulate and evaluate.

Future of VUIs

As technology continues to advance, VUIs are likely to become even more integrated into our daily lives. They are expected to play a significant role in IoT (Internet of Things) devices, smart homes, and automotive interfaces. With improvements in natural language processing and machine learning, VUIs will become more sophisticated and capable of handling complex tasks and conversations. Web designers and developers will need to stay current with VUI technology and best practices to create engaging and user-friendly voice interfaces.

Section 20.4: Augmented Reality (AR) and Virtual Reality (VR)

Augmented Reality (AR) and Virtual Reality (VR) are cutting-edge technologies that have the potential to revolutionize the way we interact with digital content and the physical world. AR enhances the real world by overlaying digital information, while VR immerses users in entirely virtual environments. These technologies offer exciting possibilities for web design and user experiences.

Augmented Reality (AR)

AR in Web Design

AR can be integrated into web design to provide unique and interactive experiences. Web AR allows users to view digital content in the real world through their device's camera, often using markers or object recognition. For example, a furniture retailer's website could offer an AR feature that allows users to see how a piece of furniture would look in their own living room.

AR Challenges and Considerations

Implementing AR on the web comes with challenges, including:

- **Compatibility:** AR experiences depend on device capabilities, so compatibility can be an issue. Designers must consider which devices and browsers support AR features.

- **User Engagement:** While AR can provide engaging experiences, it's essential to strike a balance between interactivity and usability, ensuring that AR elements enhance rather than detract from the user experience.

- **Content Creation:** Creating AR content requires specialized skills and tools, which can be a barrier for some web designers.

Virtual Reality (VR)

VR in Web Design

VR allows users to immerse themselves in virtual environments. In web design, WebVR and WebXR technologies enable VR experiences to be delivered through web browsers. This opens up opportunities for creating virtual tours, training simulations, and immersive storytelling on the web.

VR Challenges and Considerations

Designing for VR on the web presents its own set of challenges:

- **Performance:** VR experiences demand high performance to maintain immersion. Optimizing assets and interactions is crucial for a smooth experience.

- **Motion Sickness:** Some users may experience motion sickness in VR, so designers should implement best practices to reduce discomfort.

- **Accessibility:** Ensuring that VR content is accessible to all users, including those with disabilities, is a critical consideration.

Future Trends

AR and VR are still evolving, and their future in web design is promising. As hardware becomes more affordable and accessible, we can expect to see increased adoption of AR and VR on the web. These technologies will continue to shape how users interact with content, from virtual showrooms for e-commerce to educational VR experiences. Keeping up with emerging AR and VR trends will be essential for web designers looking to stay at the forefront of digital experiences.

Section 20.5: The Evolving Role of Web Designers

The role of web designers has continuously evolved alongside advancements in technology and changing user expectations. In this section, we'll explore the shifting landscape of web design and the skills that modern web designers need to stay relevant and successful.

Design Beyond Aesthetics

While aesthetics and visual design remain crucial aspects of web design, the modern web designer's responsibilities extend far beyond creating visually appealing websites. Designers must now consider user experience (UX) design, information architecture, and content strategy. They need to ensure that websites are not only beautiful but also functional and user-friendly.

Responsive and Mobile-First Design

With the proliferation of smartphones and tablets, web designers must prioritize responsive and mobile-first design. Users access websites on various devices and screen sizes, making it essential to create designs that adapt seamlessly to different platforms. Understanding media queries, flexible layouts, and mobile design principles is vital.

Accessibility and Inclusivity

Accessibility has become a central concern in web design. Designers should follow accessibility guidelines (such as WCAG) to make websites usable by people with disabilities. This includes providing alternative text for images, ensuring keyboard navigation, and designing with considerations for color contrast. Inclusive design goes beyond compliance and aims to create websites that cater to a diverse range of users.

Coding Proficiency

Modern web designers benefit from having coding skills, even if they don't write full-fledged applications. Understanding HTML, CSS, and JavaScript allows designers to communicate effectively with developers and make design decisions that align with the technical constraints of the web.

Collaboration and Communication

Effective communication and collaboration are essential skills for web designers. They often work closely with developers, content creators, and stakeholders. Clear communication helps ensure that design concepts are translated accurately into the final product and that all team members are on the same page.

Keeping Up with Trends and Tools

The web design landscape is continually evolving. Designers must stay updated with the latest design trends, tools, and technologies. This includes knowledge of design software, prototyping tools, version control systems, and design systems. Staying current with industry trends allows designers to deliver modern and competitive web experiences.

User-Centered Design

User-centered design (UCD) principles emphasize designing with the end-user in mind. Conducting user research, creating user personas, and performing usability testing are valuable techniques for ensuring that websites meet user needs and expectations. UCD helps designers create empathetic and effective designs.

Conclusion

In the ever-changing world of web design, adaptability and a commitment to lifelong learning are key. The evolving role of web designers demands a multidisciplinary approach, encompassing both technical and creative skills. By embracing these changes and continuously improving their craft, web designers can create exceptional web experiences that resonate with users in the digital age.

www.ingramcontent.com/pod-product-compliance
Lightning Source LLC
Chambersburg PA
CBHW071242050326
40690CB00011B/2231